To all the strong women that are and have been in my life.

My sweet grandmothers – one that fostered a love of exploration, one that fostered a love of food.

To Lori, my angel. Her hugs, hospitality and laughter will never be forgotten.

And of course, my number one since day one, my Mom. I'll love you forever, I'll like you for always…

Chasing Harvest Volume 1

KEVIN
O'CONNOR

Contents

Foreword

My dog's name is Kevin. I love Kevin the Dog. I also love Kevin the Human. They exist on the same continuum of good things, kind energy, love and an ongoing desire to discover new cool shit – new cool humans, dogs and even cats. Kevin is Kevin. It's a vibe, a state of mind and being.

Kevin the Human could've been a lot of things: bass player in a punk band, a dreadlocked Rasta, Lou Reed's best friend, a space cowboy...

If he had wanted to, he could've opened a great restaurant that, because of his truly singular style, would have started a lot of people talking, thus putting him on a familiar trajectory for young, gifted chefs. I met Kevin as he was preparing to do just that – launching his first restaurant. Instead he bravely chose to chase a never-ending harvest. He made two beautiful olive groves – one in Yolo County Northern California and the other in Boundary Bend, Australia – his restaurant tableau.

I've eaten a lot of food all over the world as it came with the trade in my various careers. I've also known a lot of chefs, not the least of which being the inimitable Charlie Trotter. Of all those meals, by all of those chefs, I can remember none of it in the visceral, sensual, literal way that I remember Kevin's food. My wife, Ivette says that Kevin's pumpkin enchiladas will be her last meal in this life. There it is. Kevin the Human.

This book is not a cookbook. It's not just a diary. It's not about our food porn fetish. It's about a singular human's journey across the universe.

Daniel Graeff
Cobram Estate USA

Preface

Chef-at-Large. That's me. That's who I am.

It's a title that has continued to evolve with me. I mean, now that I've heard it so many times in so many different contexts, it means different things. I don't know, just today I was thinking about different ways to explore it. It's kind of open to evolution, unlike Corporate Chef or Executive Chef. Titles with limitations that you're aware of the moment you say them to somebody.

Chef-at-Large, though… It's like, 'forget that identity of chef, executive chef, corporate chef, company chef or "culinary director"', whatever the █████ people call it. The identity and the responsibilities and the effectiveness of what we do – what I do – changes all the time.

Being malleable, being fluid, that's what it's all about.

To always be moving.

Film Selfie - Japan?

In a restaurant, you're doing the same stuff all the time. Even if you change things on the menu every day, you're still going into that restaurant and flicking on the same lights and managing the same people and looking at a similar schedule, and you're still worried about the bottom line every night. You're still worried about who the ███is coming in, or what that VIP is doing. But Chef-at-Large is… one day you're worried if you're actually going to get on the plane and make it, and then other days it's about gathering ingredients, discovering what's in season, or just generally getting your shit together.

If I was stuck doing the same thing for an entire year and then we were like, 'Okay, now let's do this', it would take so much time to adjust. But I've adjusted to doing something different all the time. And doing something different all the time is now the norm.

I don't think I've cooked the same thing once, really, in this position, whereas in a restaurant, all you do is repeat a dish all night. You might throw something new on the menu or run a special – it's something unique to the night but you're still going to make it 40 times – whereas with this… we gear up and serve, they eat it, and then it's probably not going to happen ever again.

So it's not just me that always moving, it's the food along with it.

And yet, in among all that movement there's one constant – harvest. It's what pulls me around the globe every year. It's my moon. Being Chef-at-Large for an olive growing company that has groves in each hemisphere – in both my native California and Victoria, Australia – means six months of fall, the most important time of the year, twice a year.

It's perpetual harvest.

'Cooking is an art; it demands hard and sometimes distasteful work, but on the whole, it is the creative side that prevails.'

Constance Spry

Chapter 1

Home

US Harvest.

A good restaurant concept should breathe the breath of the chef but the body of it should be everybody else. But with our harvest, the responsibilities are greater.

The olive harvest here at home in California for me is weeks of non-stop entertaining and cooking. You're entertaining up until you go to sleep – you're out by the campfire and drinking with people and you're still on your game, then you tuck everybody in and say goodnight, then wake up before they wake up. It's almost like being a parent.

It's fun. I love it. And not in the ways you might think. I love creating these experiences, the hospitality that's involved and all the help I receive along the way. I try to be a driving force in curating and nurturing that experience – to be the shaman of food and fun.

Here in California I get the chance to curate a menu based on what's in season, and I have pretty much everything available because we're in the most abundant time, plus I've got all these relationships with these farmers and producers that I've forged. I can start prepping in advance, I know where I need to go foraging for things and I know where to get shit from. I know exactly what's going to be tasting good at this time of year to the point where, sometimes, it's too much. There's just too many colors on the palette and I don't know what I'm going to paint.

Aside from the food, what's missing has been kind of what's growing more and more each year. It's that communal aspect, and we're getting closer to it, though it's hard to get a bunch of strangers together and have them be best friends.

We've succeeded at that on some level, but at the same time, you gotta kind of compare it to what you would experience if you were to go camping with your friends. Do you guys get the most from the experience that happens around the campfire, or is it from those moments that happens around a table, when you're cooking for your friends? And how much can you juice out of a person to have that happen in three days? You know, how many plates do we have to spin to create that? And if you're spinning all those plates is it still 'authentic' enough to create that experience? So, it's a balance between creating that in such a short amount of time and still being authentic.

I love to show people California, our home. There's just nothing better.

and how we get down

Chasing Harvest

This was the first California Harvest I've had a real kitchen.

I mean, real kitchen might be pushing it. It's not finished or put together and done or anything. But it is a kitchen. The last few years I've been cooking out of my house and a break room with a problematic oven and a ~~blowing~~ sink that flooded all the time. That was the worst.

It was weird being without a kitchen for so long because a chef without a kitchen just doesn't seem... relevant. Having space to ~~work and create that~~ call your own is really important. Plus, it definitely helps you cook for a bunch of people.

I feel like I'm back in something. It's definitely not a restaurant, but it had been so long and you get so wrapped up in the shit that you're doing for whoever, whatever, that you don't really realize that you're so constrained without a kitchen until you get one and then you're like, 'Oh yeah! This is what it's like to be able to cook and explore and experiment, to have your own space and something that produces some creative flow.'

Without that kitchen there were times I felt I was putting everything on pause as a chef – or maybe just what I think it's important to be, and to do, and to have as a chef – so now I feel like I'm just kind of getting started again and becoming re-inspired and falling in love with what I do for the ~~fucking~~ billionth time.

It's cool to continually do that. Loving food so much and falling in love with what you do so many times that you go through falling in love with it, and not necessarily falling out of love with it but kind of just… getting used to it. And then when you're able to fall in <u>love</u> with it again you're so impressed that you're actually just able to do that. That after 14, 15, 16 years you're still finding new ways to love food. To love cooking. To love entertaining. To love doing rad shit for people.

So yeah, the new kitchen was pretty cool.

The beginnings of the hearth

Native Californian service

Makes approximately 20 griddle cakes

Griddle cakes

1 cup (125 g/4½ oz) acorn flour
1 cup (150 g/5½ oz) all-purpose (plain) flour
2 teaspoons baking powder
1 teaspoon salt
1½–2 cups (375–500 ml/12½–17 fl oz) whole
   (full-cream) milk (depending on your flour's
   absorption rate)
2 eggs
½ cup (175 ml/6 fl oz) honey
¼ cup (60 ml/2 fl oz) extra-virgin olive oil,
   plus extra for cooking

To serve

1 x 1 oz (30 g) tin of Sterling caviar
4 tablespoons cured salmon caviar
extra-virgin olive oil
2 tablespoons finely chopped chives
1 handful of edible buds and blossoms, such
   as marigold petals and blossoming arugula
   (rocket) buds

At one of the first Californian harvests I was doing a walk-through of an olive grove with Adam, the president of operations here in the States and our main man in the groves. After a while walking and talking we decided on this beautiful spot for our harvest lunch, under some huge ancient oak trees on top of this hill.

Anyway, for the meal itself I was looking for ingredient inspiration from within the area and in the twenty minutes or so we were chatting there about forty acorns landed on me, which I took as a sign that they had to be on the menu. So I made some acorn flour (which I don't suggest anyone does because it's a huge pain in the ass – you'd be better off buying it) and used it to make the acorn griddle cakes that would be a part of my local, less fancy take on a fine dining caviar service. I called it a native Californian caviar service because along with the acorns I'd also used the roe of fish that were native to California and then topped the lot off with wild buds and blossoms.

Start with the griddle cakes. Combine the dry ingredients in a small bowl. In a separate, larger bowl, mix together the milk, eggs, honey and olive oil. Slowly incorporate the dry ingredients into the wet until a spoonable batter forms.
   Heat a griddle or a large cast-iron skillet over medium–high heat and add a drizzle of olive oil. With a spoon or a small ladle, begin to make 1 inch (2.5 cm) rounds with the batter. Cook for 1 minute or until bubbling on the edges, then flip and leave to cook for another 1 minute or until deep golden brown on each side.
   To serve, arrange the griddle cakes on a platter. In a bowl, very gently stir the two caviars together with a drizzle of olive oil. Pile the caviar mixture on top of the warm cakes, scatter over the chives and flower buds and finish everything off with another drizzle of oil. Enjoy immediately.

Grilled eggplant and snake beans with turmeric

Serves 10–12

4 eggplants (aubergines), cut into quarters
    and scored
1 bunch of snake (yardlong) beans, tips trimmed
sea salt
2 tablespoons extra-virgin olive oil
8 shiso or basil leaves, torn into small pieces

Turmeric glaze

1 cup (250 ml/8½ fl oz) freshly squeezed
    orange juice
3 tablespoons honey
1½ teaspoons ground turmeric
1 whole dried Thai or árbol chili
1 teaspoon sea salt

Although I served this up in California, this dish takes inspiration from both Thailand and Australia; it's funny seeing the food I cook at home evolve from these places and experiences. If you haven't had grilled snake beans (Chinese long beans) like this before you should definitely give them a try. Being large, they are easy to pick up with tongs – just toss them with olive oil and chuck them on the grill for a very different flavor experience. The turmeric glaze, which ~~I developed in Australia, is something I thought a lot of the folk at this particular lunch would enjoy as they were pretty healthy eaters, and it pulls the different elements of the dish together nicely~~ STUPID

Fire up your grill (barbecue) to a medium–high heat.

Salt the eggplant pieces heavily and leave them to rest in a colander placed in the sink for at least 15 minutes to draw out the moisture, then gently squeeze them between paper towels. Transfer to a mixing bowl with the snake beans, olive oil and a pinch of salt. Toss to coat.

Lay the snake beans and eggplant pieces, cut side down, on the hot grill plate. Cook for 10–15 minutes, turning the eggplant and snake beans occasionally, until heavy grill marks are achieved.

While the veg are grilling, make the turmeric glaze. Bring the orange juice, honey, turmeric, dried chili and salt to a boil in a small saucepan. Reduce the heat to a simmer and leave it to bubble away until it's thickened and glossy, about 25 minutes.

Transfer the grilled veg to a large mixing bowl together with the shiso or basil leaves and pour over the reduced glaze. Toss everything together well and serve immediately.

Home

Poached salmon, bitter greens and sweet herbs

Serves 8

1 × 2 lb (900 g) salmon fillet
kosher salt
4 cups (1 litre/34 fl oz) extra-virgin olive oil
1 tablespoon white peppercorns
1 tablespoon fennel seeds
2 lemons, 1 sliced into rings, 1 juiced
3 fresh bay leaves
1 radicchio head
2 frisée lettuce heads, dark green tips trimmed
1 cup (25 g/1 oz) flat-leaf parsley leaves
½ cup (15 g/½ oz) tarragon leaves
½ cup (15 g/½ oz) chervil or dill fronds
fresh extra-virgin olive oil, for drizzling
pinch of salt
a few spoonfuls of aïoli (see below), to serve
sourdough bread, to serve

Extra-virgin olive oil aïoli (Makes approx.
  2 cups/500 g)

1 cup (250 ml/8½ fl oz) mild extra-virgin olive oil
2 tablespoons lemon juice
3 tablespoons reserved chickpea water (aquafaba)
1 teaspoon Dijon mustard
pinch of salt
1 garlic clove, lightly crushed but still whole

This dish evolved as a way to welcome people to harvest. The first time I made it, people were arriving at different times and I wanted something that was easy to execute and wouldn't wilt or die or need to be reheated or anything. So, the salmon sides were poached in a ton of really fresh olive oil together with all sorts of aromatics, and I strained off some of that oil to make the aïoli. The salmon was then able to kind of sit there at room temperature in that poaching oil and when people arrived I would kind of cut them off chunks of it, toss a little salad together with some bitter greens and some sweet herbs to kind of play off each other, and finish the whole lot off with a giant dollop of aïoli and a victory drizzle of first harvest over the top.

Without the salmon, this aïoli is the base of so many dressings, sauces and salads. I also regularly find myself reaching into the fridge at midnight to dip celery sticks, chunks of bread or carrots into a container of it, often doctored with chopped herbs, chili sauce or cracked pepper and lemon zest.

Let the salmon come to room temperature and salt heavily with kosher salt. Set aside.

While the salt is permeating the salmon, bring the olive oil, peppercorns, fennel seeds, lemon rings and bay leaves up to medium heat in a wide saucepan. Let the aromatics simmer in the oil for about 10 minutes, then carefully lower the salmon into the olive oil, making sure it's fully submerged. Leave to poach in the oil over very low heat for 15–20 minutes, or until less orange and more light pink and slightly firm to the touch. Remove from the heat and set aside (the salmon will keep, resting in the oil at room temperature, for up to 1 hour before serving).

While the salmon is cooking, prep the salad. Chop the radicchio and frisée into small pieces, then transfer to a mixing bowl together with the lemon juice, herbs and a drizzle of fresh olive oil. Toss together well, season with a pinch of salt and set aside.

To make the aïoli, add all the ingredients, except the garlic clove, to a jar and blend with a stick blender until smooth. Use a rubber spatula, transfer the emulsion to a small container with a lid, press the garlic clove into the mixture and refrigerate for at least 1 hour before using. (The aïoli will keep in the fridge for up to 1 week, just be sure to remove and discard the garlic clove on day 2).

When ready to eat, remove the salmon from the oil and break into large chunks. Divide among plates and top with spoonfuls of aïoli and a drizzle of fresh oil. Serve with the

04/12/2010

I've found inspiration again, but on a different level.

I was so inspired in the past and so worried that I had maybe lost it for so long, but it's been coming back piece by piece, and so many pieces are there now. And I know now what I didn't know then.

I really feel like this coming year we've got so much going on, but I feel confident about all of it and feel like we've got – or I've got – a decent handle on how to do a lot of this. Last year, the year before, I didn't really know what the fuck I was doing. I had no idea what I was doing the first year I was with Cobram and doing this whole thing.

It's not like we weren't working hard, but it was just figuring how to make it effective. We still are – I mean, it's something that you always keep working on, but this year I feel like there's a clear vision. Things are picking up and we're starting to stand up on the surfboard and look back at this big wave that's about to just fucking annihilate, and there are those that are with us, they're about to shred, and there are those, like we've seen, that have just kind of been slurped up by the big foamy wave.

There are moments where I can't believe I'm still surfing and that I'm going to ride this wave. You're like, okay, I'm going to ride this out. But I've still got to ride it out. And I'm sure after that there's going to be more waves, much bigger waves. You just keep riding bigger waves and then you die.

And that's life.

The Clash Ghetto Defendant

Chasing Harvest

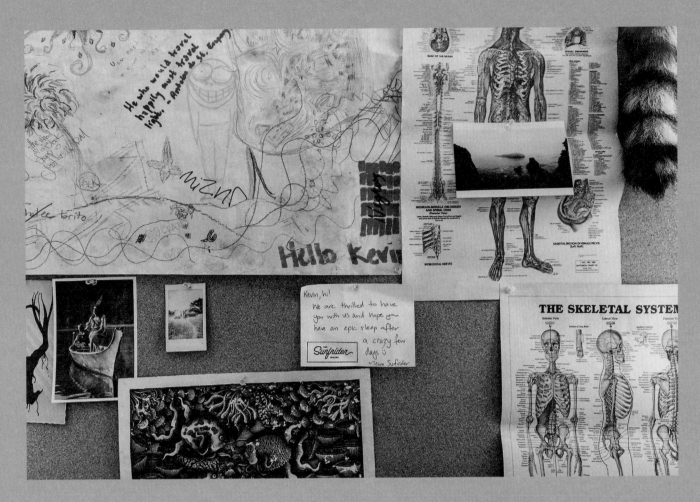

1. [The Beginnings]

I've always loved food, on some level. At first, when I was a kid, I fell in love with the theater of it, and I'd ask for tours of the kitchen at every restaurant that we went to as a family, even if it was part of a chain.

Most of the time they would say, 'Dude, you're, like, eight. We can't even legally take you back', but there was one place where we got a tour every time. It was a nicer restaurant called Mace's (it was owned by Bruce Mace, who was a friend of my dad's) and we'd go in and get taken care of a little bit. Right outside the kitchen there was this big zebra pelt on the wall and I remember thinking, 'this is a ▓▓▓▓ cool place'.

I mean, it wasn't extreme fine dining or anything (obviously, because my dad was bringing his 'heathens') but it was still a nice place. A legit kitchen, great wine list, decent menu. You know, your basic middle-of-the-road American fine dining place where you can get steak, lobster and probably some nice pasta dishes. I thought it was just so fancy when I was little.

And going out to dinner there was always cool. The chef would come out and say hello, the owner would come over and pop a bottle of champagne open at the table, or something like that, and we'd be eating what seemed to be the fanciest food ever... because it was – I mean, at that point in my life, it really was the fanciest shit I'd ever eaten. You know, it was probably like 30 minutes from the house but it seemed like we always had to go on a ▓▓▓▓ road trip to get to this place.

I remember the theater of it all started with mom and dad getting ready. My parents would always play music and have drinks while getting ready. My dad would make a cocktail while my mom was working away and producing all sorts of smells out of her bathroom – perfume and hair spray and... you know, it was the early nineties so lots... And they'd play Zeppelin on these old-school speakers that we had, with all the dials and all sorts of shit. They used to play CDs. I remember that as a kid, playing a lot of music – a lot of eighties butt-rock, Van Halen and Mötley Crüe, and running around the house beating shit up to Soundgarden.

Anyway, they'd always take time to get ready and enjoy themselves. I realize now that they were just really good at relaxing and separating themselves from work. At enjoying their family, their home.

SPOON MAN

Zeppelin – Physical Graffiti

Always sleepy

Hey Dad

When my brother & I had a reggae group

American River by my house

Later, my parents used to try to talk me out of cooking. Not talk me out of cooking, but talk me out of pursuing it as an actual career, knowing that it would be extremely difficult to make it or to be at all successful. And their ideas of success in the culinary world were the things that I despised. Working for some big hotel chain, working on a cruise ship – those kind of uninspired food factories that have benefits.

I remember there being a lot of times that I had to tell them, basically, to just fuck off and hang on 10 years. I think it changed by the time I was a chef at Blackbird and doing cool things and getting into publications and making a name for myself… or maybe it was before Blackbird, at the first Treehouse dinner, where I had to throw together a pop-up restaurant so that Sacramento magazine could cover it, and my mom and brother helped serve and my dad helped in the kitchen.

But I'm getting ahead of myself. Where was I? Oh yeah, the theatrics of food. It's what first attracted me to cooking, and it's still the bit I'm doing a lot of now. Curating an experience rather than just feeding some people. It's what makes it fun and it's what's made me successful without knowing it – creating a mood, building new memories while playing on existing ones. It's what makes it all mean something, I guess.

the A1 taco spot

Chargrilled creamed corn with wild and tame mushrooms

Serves 4–6

8 sweetcorn ears, husks and silk removed
3 tablespoons extra-virgin olive oil, plus extra
  for drizzling
1½ cups (375 ml/12½ fl oz) heavy (thick/double)
  cream
½ cup (125 ml/4 fl oz) crème fraîche
2 tablespoons red miso paste
1½–2 lb (680–900 g) wild and cultivated
  mushrooms (such as chanterelle, shiitake
  and maitake mushrooms)
sea salt
basil and chives, to serve

I first made this dish in an olive grove in California and – if I'm honest – I was kind of winging it. I put the corn cobs over the fire to let them blister up nicely before cutting them off and stirring them into the cream and crème fraîche to add another layer of smokiness. I've always loved corn and chanterelles together and the basil and fresh olive oil really sets the combination off. I've made a lot of different versions of creamed corn with mushrooms, but this has been my favorite so far.

Fire up a charcoal grill (barbecue) and let the coals get nice and hot.

Arrange the corn cobs on a rack above the hot coals and cook, turning occasionally, for 20 minutes or until most of the kernels are dark brown and caramelized.

Cut the roasted kernels from the cobs into a small camp oven. Scrape the pulp from the cobs with the tip of a spoon and add them to the oven with the corn, then stir in the cream, crème fraiche and miso. Leave the mixture to bubble away, stirring occasionally, until it has thickened to a porridge-like consistency.

Meanwhile, place a cast-iron pan directly onto the coals. Add the olive oil and the mushrooms to the pan, season with a little salt and cook, stirring, until the mushrooms are nicely golden brown

To serve, divide the miso creamed corn among plates, top with the roasted mushrooms and finish with a final drizzle of olive oil and a scattering of freshly cut chives and torn basil leaves.

Pumpkin enchiladas, mole Californio and coriander pesto

Makes 12 enchiladas

2 kabocha squash (Japanese pumpkins)
   or Kent pumpkins
¾ cup (185 ml/6 fl oz) extra-virgin olive oil
salt
12 large tortillas (use your favorites),
   1 torn into small pieces
finely sliced red onion, to serve

Mole Californio

4 dried ancho chiles, ribs and seeds removed
4 dried guajillo chiles, ribs and seeds removed
½ teaspoon black peppercorns
½ teaspoon whole allspice berries
¼ teaspoon whole cloves
1 cinnamon stick
4 cups (1 litre/34 fl oz) vegetable stock
1 onion, diced
2 tablespoons extra-virgin olive oil, plus extra
   for drizzling
1 tablespoon sesame seeds
1 cup (220 g/8 oz) whole cherry tomatoes
1 garlic clove
¼ cup (30 g/1 oz) golden raisins
3 tablespoons honey
⅓ cup (40 g/1½ oz) bittersweet (dark)
   chocolate chips
¼ teaspoon smoked paprika
¼ teaspoon dried achiote (annatto) powder
sea salt

Pesto

1 cup (150 g/5½ oz) toasted pepitas (pumpkin
   seeds), plus extra to serve
½ bunch of flat-leaf parsley, roughly chopped
½ bunch of cilantro (coriander), roughly chopped,
   plus extra to serve
juice of 4 limes
1 cup (250 ml/8½ fl oz) extra-virgin olive oil

These enchiladas have been kind of a staple at harvest and are very much my idea of what California food should be. The pumpkins are roasted in the fire, then the filling is scooped out, mixed with olive oil and rolled into these beautiful green chili tortillas, while the pesto is really simple – it's just the seeds from the pumpkin blended with some greens. The mole is a Californian riff on a Mexican mole *coloradito* with lots of local ingredients incorporated into it. It takes a lot of time and is ~~kind of~~ a pain in the ass to make, but it's worth it.

If you think about it, the dish itself is so simple – it's just some pumpkin inside of a tortilla with two sauces. But putting some time, effort and love into the sauces and roasting the pumpkin properly really makes for a simple, impressive and madly delicious dish. My friend Dan's wife, Ivette (who ~~fucking~~ knows her food) actually said that these enchiladas are the thing she would eat on her death bed, which is one of the best compliments I've ever received.

Preheat the oven to 350°F (180°C).
   Cut ¼ in (5 mm) off the top and the bottom of each pumpkin to help keep them level, then cut them into quarters, keeping the seeds intact for roasting. Place the pumpkin quarters, skin side down, on a baking sheet, pour over 1/2 cup (125 ml/4 fl oz) of olive oil, season with salt and bake for 1 hour, or until the pumpkin flesh is soft and easily punctured with a fork.
   While the pumpkin is roasting, make the mole. Arrange the chiles on a baking sheet and toast in the 350°F (180°C) oven for 7–10 minutes, or until very aromatic. Leave to cool, then rip the tops off the chiles and shake out the seeds. Tear the chiles into pieces, removing any seeds that may be left, and set aside until needed.
   Meanwhile, add the peppercorns, allspice, cloves and cinnamon to a saucepan set over low heat and toast for 5–7 minutes, or until very aromatic. Add the stock to the pan and bring to a boil, then reduce the heat and leave to simmer for at least 20 minutes, or until the stock is well infused with the spices.
   In a separate large saucepan, sauté the onion in the olive oil until soft and translucent. Add the sesame seeds, tomatoes, garlic, raisins and torn tortilla pieces and cook on low heat, stirring occasionally, until the tomatoes have softened and begun to release their juices. Strain the spice-infused stock into the pan, bring to a simmer and cook for 5–10 minutes to allow the flavors to marry. Stir the honey and torn chile pieces into the mixture, transfer to a blender and blend together, starting on low speed, gradually working up to high and adding the chocolate

chips, smoked paprika, achiote, a few pinches of salt and a drizzle of oil as you go, until everything is smooth and well combined. (Be careful to place a towel over the hole in the lid of the blender as you go, so the steam has a place to escape). Taste and season again with salt, if needed, then set aside.

Remove the pumpkin quarters from the oven and leave to cool slightly before removing the seeds and membrane, reserving roughly a quarter of the total amount for the mole. Gently scoop the pumpkin flesh away from the skins into a mixing bowl, add the remaining 1/4 cup (60 ml/2 fl oz) olive oil to the bowl with a good pinch of salt and roughly mash together with a spoon. Set aside.

For the pesto, put the toasted pepitas, herbs and lime juice in the blender with a big pinch of salt. Blend together on high adding the olive oil in a slow steady stream until all the oil has been incorporated and the pesto is smooth

To put the enchiladas together, coat a ceramic baking dish with a drizzle of olive oil. Working one tortilla at a time, spoon a generous quantity of the pumpkin (about ¼ cup/60 ml) filling down the length of the tortilla, then roll it up and place it seam-side down in the oiled dish. (Be careful not to add too much filling – the enchilada should be full, but the pumpkin should not be oozing out of the sides.) Repeat this step until you have a full dish of enchiladas.

Brush half the mole evenly over the top of the enchiladas. (The remainder will keep in an airtight container in the fridge for up to 1 week for a repeat dish or for the boar shoulder recipe on page 100). Cover the dish with foil and bake in the oven for 15–20 minutes, or until the center is hot.

To serve, remove the enchiladas from the dish and divide among plates. Top with a few spoonfuls of the pesto, a scattering of cilantro, some additional pumpkin seeds and some finely sliced red onion.

12/4/2014

I had a good time with some food today. I also decided I should start keeping a record of these good times that I have with food.

I write a lot of shit down, but it's always jumbled up with random 'get your shit together' notes, prep lists and scratched out ideas. That's not to say that whatever I start in this comp book – that I've already ripped three pages out of to pretend that it's new – will be organized. That would be kidding myself.

But at least it's a start.

Anyway, I had a play around with some turnips, which I roasted in cascara – the dried skins of coffee cherries. I coated them with olive oil, surrounded them with the cascara and baked them in a hot oven until tender. After cleaning them off, I sliced them into rounds and served them up with rounds of pear, some mustard flowers and the blanched white lengths of a spring onion, filling in the gaps with an Asian malt vinegar made with barley and sorghum, and then a drizzle of olive oil.

To improve this dish, I'm not sure if I'd add another element. The onions could use work – maybe I could dress or age them? The Asian pear could be compressed, or something other than raw. I suppose, if I had to add something to the dish, perhaps some puffed barley or sorghum grains, or sprouts? I had turnip greens, which I was going to use as a garnish along with the mustard flowers, but I rather liked the aesthetic as it was. I suppose I could experiment with thickening the vinegar or making a sauce out of it, though.

And what olive oil would be best?

5/12/2014

WHACKY IDEA

What if a kitchen had secondary stations or assignments? For example, the garde manger chef would be in charge of all greens, sprouts etc. Another cook would be in charge of the dairy station, making sure that there is always items like cultured butter, buttermilk, crème fraîche, yogurt etc. The 'Pantry' station would handle most preserve and the root cellar, the 'Meat Locker' would, of course, go to the meat cook. Perhaps a 'Poisonnier' position would mean aging fish, making fumés, vinegars and salts from the bones etc. You could urge each station manager to really take ownership of each station, presenting one project a week/month with their products. You could give each station a name, relative to what is important to that station – milk, plants, meat or oil, for example).

It could be pretty cool…

Misfits - Static Age (one of the greatest albums)

2. [Masque & Before]

I was at Masque when I was 17. It wasn't the first restaurant I worked in, but it was the first serious restaurant I worked in, and it was the first restaurant that I had the love, and the fear instilled so fucking hard at the same time.

By that time I knew cooking like this was what I wanted to do, but I was terrified every day I went to work. It's the first place I got slapped across the face by the sous chef. I had to watch his risotto when he walked away – it was a risotto that we were using rabbit stock in and I had put lobster stock in it when he walked away, because we had a lobster risotto on the menu, too.

It was a really fucking great restaurant and I had no business working there at all. I showed up to that restaurant pretty much every day when they first opened, with my shitty resume. I was like, 'Hey, I'm Kevin. I've worked in these two restaurants washing dishes and being a prep cook, basically. I'm in high school, I like dirt bikes and I play football!' Until one day the chef just said, "All right, dude, what's your schedule? We can work you in." They needed some help. So I worked my way through all those stations at Masque as a 17-year-old.

Masque was when I realized that I wanted to pursue the knowledge and the professionalism that's involved in fine dining. It was like, 'this is how it's fucking done', I'm not going to slap steak and potatoes at bar 'n' grills or anything like that.

Before Masque, I had worked at a few places. Including Z's Bistro and for some British lady as her little sous chef at another restaurant.

I can't remember the name. I just remember she yelled at me a lot and she always called me a vegetable.

'Oh, you ~~fucking~~ vegetable.'

After that I'd gone to the Country Club, where I worked at the appetizer station. I was 16, I think. That was cool. The Country Club was ~~fucking~~ fun – it was the first place I got super rascally. I went to school with the kids who would drive the golf carts and they were in the basement, so after work, after they had tournaments at the golf course, we would go down to the basement and clean out the rest of the beer from the kegs. Because they would have the golf carts with the kegs on them going around at the tournament and they wouldn't return them, they'd bring the golf carts back to the garage.

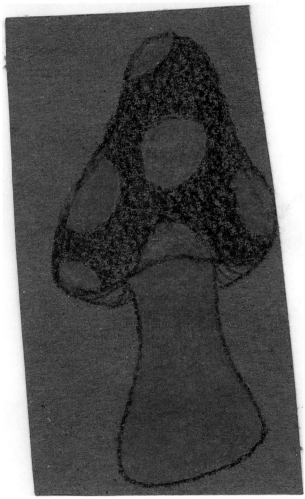

Sacramento's Sunday Market

And so, we would just clear out the kegs and make this mix of beer and then take the big golf carts out. We had developed these secret paths throughout the golf course in the trees and stuff, that had bumps and jumps for the golf carts. So we made this golf cart course. We'd get drunk on beer and play baseball with golf clubs and take the golf carts through these courses that we made, and I'd bring them leftover food and stuff.

It was there I started realizing that I was really into food. There were some cool servers there who were 19, 20, 21, 22, who were into food and wine. I'd go over to their house afterwards and smoke weed and hang out and talk about and taste wine and food. They would make food, they would make pasta from scratch or something. They were these ... they were just cool. They were kids who liked food and lived alone. They weren't living with their parents and they weren't in high school, they really just enjoyed the good shit in life. They brewed beer. They always had a ton of weed, which you don't have at high school. They were able to smoke in their house. Like, holy shit.

They also had a ton of cool books. Friends in high school were never really like, 'Hey here, check this book out.' In high school, even if a friend did that I'd probably have said something along the lines of ~~Your mum and dad are dickheads and you're an idiot~~ But those guys read stuff and they compared notes.

They loved music too. I mean, music's been important in every restaurant kitchen I've worked in, pretty much, but those guys would get together and cook and hang out and listen to Zeppelin and Hendrix and talk about Janis Joplin and touch on all those old classics. I grew up on it and I knew about Led Zeppelin and all that, but I never really just hung out and listened to John Bonham and drank wine like that.

Those guys were rad.

Hendrix - Axis as bold as love

After that, I started working in downtown Sacramento before I moved down here, and quickly became part of the kitchen crew at Mason's. It was a bit of a pirate crew, with a lot of partying afterwards.

Sacramento was a cool new world, and my homie Tyler lived down there. We agreed to move down in the same summer, but I ended up lagging a bit and leaving him hanging on the moving out thing. To make it up to him, I frequently hung out and basically hijacked his apartment to be a general 18-year-old downtown shithead. Before I moved, I'd go to his house all the time after work, or whatever was going on, to cook or to crash. I remember he had his... he slept on an air mattress, and my first serious girlfriend and I kicked him out of the place to be alone together. We ended up popping it and for weeks after he slept engulfed in this half-deflated taco-shaped mattress.

Sorry Tyler

Summer is gathering elderberries

Mason's was, besides Masque, another one of the really influential kitchens that I worked in. That was the first restaurant I worked at when I was living alone and kind of embracing this lifestyle of a young cook. I moved downtown in 2008, which is when everything turned upside down and restaurants were closing left and right. I was young enough and scrappy enough to be malleable enough to stick through it with Mason's, you know. Hours were cut and it was shitty, and I was like, 'all right, I'm already broke – I'm ~~████~~ 8'. My parents still paid my phone bill probably and my brother gave me weed to sell, so I was fine. But other people weren't, and I didn't realize how lucky I was to have stuck that out. When things weren't so fucking bad I was still there and I'd been there long enough to learn about the place and work my way up.

After Mason's I went and helped open MiX kind of as a sous chef. That was when I was 19. They didn't know if they wanted to be a club or a bar or what. The bar and the club kind of won out, rather than the small plates lounge or whatever they attempted to label it when they had first opened. I dunno, perhaps they tried too early and Sacramento would get it now, but back then Sacramento wasn't really ready for a dope small plates lounge with music at night.

Hey!
– THE PIXIES

Friends from Riverdog farm

3\21\19

I tried a pretty good vino at work today. Well, several actually, but the one I'm talking about (and which I'm drinking another glass of now) was a Barossa Valley shiraz.

A little taste of Australia back home.

It's a big, bold and meaty wine. Lots of ~~strong~~ blue and red berry action going on. A touch of French oak. Oh yeah, it's nice. ~~something~~ ~~something~~ Light, soft tannins. Not too crazy.

The texture's really rad, so I want to pair it with something very textural – something layered like filo dough with a lamb tartare on top with heaps of fresh marjoram. Or maybe even something with fried quinoa…?

Either way, I want texture with it really bad. That's something people don't explore enough in wine pairings – texture. Texture's so important. Texture's everything.

My lube, my liege

Treehouse just sort of spiraled out of nothing. It started with me thinking, 'hey, I'm just gonna cook for people and invite people over to my house for dinner every once in a while and, you know, it'd be smart if I started charging them a little bit so I'm not broke from having them over and so I can make some cooler food.'

Then I thought, 'Hey, I should start buying some wine. You know what? Maybe I'll pair this wine with these dishes.' I wasn't even old enough to buy wine, but I was having ~~fucking~~ wine-pairing dinners at my house.

Anyway, the word spread and that was when Mary-Beth from Sacramento magazine reached out and asked if she could come to my pop-up restaurant. <u>I had to google what a pop-up restaurant was, because I didn't know.</u> There was none of that shit going on in Sacramento back then. Absolutely nothing. So I threw something together; that first time my mom and brother helped serve and my dad helped in the kitchen. The magazine covered it and it went from there.

My brother and I had a lot of fun times in that house. We lived in squalor and would go to extreme lengths to clean up before I had people come over for dinner, who were then paying like a hundred bucks to come eat at my house that the day before was a ~~fucking~~ stoner pad.

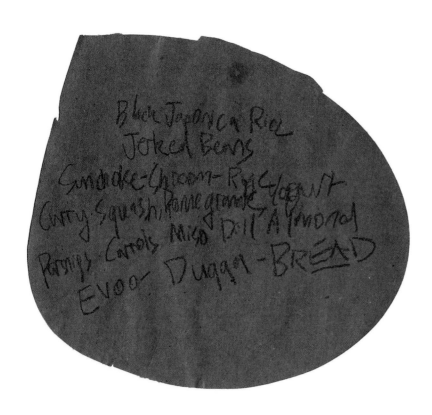

Geeked out on a sci-fi themed dinner.
A different theme inspired each course.

X-Ray Spex - Iam a Poseur

In fact, there were lots of times I made people stay outside and put snacks and beer outside while I made my brother clean up his shit. So people would hang out on that big front porch and I would just give them peanuts and Stellas before doing a 12-course dinner. ~~Wmmmmmmmmmmmm~~ Peanuts and Stellas, I'm in a Slayer shirt and we're going to have a 12-course dinner later, but right now you guys hang out on the front porch. And they thought it was so cool. They thought it was this great reveal when you'd finally slide open the pocket doors and let them into this old craftsman home and show them this dining room with doors on jack stands covered in paper with colored pencils and crayons and mix-matched plates, along with this random fucking horrible art that they thought was cool.

Something was working, though. A lot of the people who took part in those dinners and those who helped out have gone on to do cool shit, and a lot of people I met there have become people I view as lifelong friends. It also obviously put me up on the stand as a chef in Sacramento, which is why I got the job at the Blackbird, where I was promoted to chef de cuisine before we even opened, because the old chef got caught stealing company money to buy drugs – and that gave me the chance to cook so much cool shit, not think about food costs and burn myself out hard.

But that's another story.

Popcorn stories

I think that I love popcorn as much as I do because it reminds me of my grandma. She had this beautiful old red cast-iron pot (which she ended up passing down to me) that was the most beaten up thing that I had ever seen – it looked like it had been dragged behind a truck for twenty years – but it made the best popcorn ever.

Grandma was the first person I ever saw make popcorn in a pot over the stove. We would just melt ridiculous amounts of butter (I obviously use olive oil now because the amount of popcorn I eat would mean I'd be consuming a stick of butter every other night) and we would hang out and drink tea or apple cider, watch a movie and nosh on this awesome popcorn. She got it perfect every time and even as a kid I was just so impressed that there were never any kernels left over, which I think is more about knowing your pot rather than having the right pot. It's about having this sixth popcorn sense, which I think I'm getting close to having.

Later, when Treehouse first started, before it blew up into this monster that I didn't know how to control, it was just me cooking for homeys in my house. Fast forward a year or so later and we were selling tickets for 100, 120 bucks a person. Now, that might sound like a lot, but I needed to be able to buy all that shit and serve it, not to mention give the money to my brother to buy the wine – something that I couldn't do as I wasn't even 21 at that point.

With Treehouse, I really wanted to de-class this 'classy' event, to disrupt that fine dining experience, and one of the ways that I did that was by not letting people into our house at first. Instead I'd have them sit out on our front porch with an ice chest full of shit beer – Stellas, Buds… you know, literally gas station beer that I would buy from a gas station that wouldn't ID me. So people would eat popcorn (which I loved), crack peanuts and drink shit beer on my front porch until I was ready for them. They didn't know what the fuck they were getting into at that point, but they were definitely ready for something.

Oxheart tartare

Serves 4

1 beef/ox heart, trimmed, cleaned and finely chopped
½ shallot, finely diced
1 tablespoon chopped capers
1 teaspoon sriracha chili sauce
2 teaspoons Dijon mustard
juice of 1 lemon
⅓ cup (80 ml/2½ fl oz) extra-virgin olive oil,
    plus extra to serve
sea salt and freshly cracked black pepper
½ cup (15 g/½ oz) chopped flat-leaf parsley
¼ cup (10 g/¼ oz) chopped oregano
1 tablespoon sherry vinegar

To serve

1 egg yolk
grilled sourdough crostini or crackers

Treehouse was a bit of a shit show. I didn't really know what I was doing and I think that was what was so exciting to some people. People would show up at six or seven and be locked outside until I was ready for them at eight, then I'd let them in and keep hitting them with courses until almost one in the morning. It was in this bachelor pad that we lived in that was just a fucking wreck.

At the time when I started, I was really into offal and those other bits and bobs of the animal that we didn't really get to highlight in the fine dining restaurant that I was working in, and what's better than raw heart to an excited twenty-year-old kid? This dish took a lot of forms but here it is with the classic tartare preparation because, well, you've got to love the classics, and cleaning those ox hearts and chopping them was always a project I really enjoyed. I remember one pop-up I did in a space a vegan café let me use for the night. The menu focused on offal, ironically, and I came down into their kitchen to offer them a plate of this tartare. They nearly asked my guests and me to leave immediately. Greeting people with raw heart probably isn't the move I'd make now, but then it was just me cooking from… my heart.

Add the chopped beef heart, shallot, capers, chili sauce, mustard, lemon juice, 2 tablespoons of olive oil, a few cracks of black pepper and a pinch of sea salt to a bowl and mix everything together well. Taste and adjust the seasoning if necessary.

In a separate bowl, mix together the chopped herbs and vinegar with the remaining ¼ cup (60 ml/2 fl oz) olive oil.

To serve, press the tartare evenly into 3 inch (7.5 cm) ring molds or pile it neatly onto plates, spoon over the herb mixture and top each with an egg yolk. Drizzle a little extra olive oil around each tartare before serving, being sure to mix the egg yolk into the tartare with a fork before eating. Serve with grilled bread or crackers.

AM I DEMON!
- DANZIG

Sour cream and onion sturgeon

Serves 4

3 red onions, trimmed, halved and finely sliced
   on a mandolin or with a very sharp knife
salt
4 x 8 oz (220 g) sturgeon fillets, sprinkled all over
   with salt and refrigerated for 4–6 hours
4 cups (1 litre/34 oz) whole milk
2 garlic cloves, smashed
1 medium leek, white and pale-green portion only,
   sliced in half lengthwise with some root attached
1 bay leaf
4 thyme sprigs
1 teaspoon white peppercorns, lightly toasted
3 tablespoons crème fraîche
1 bunch of chives, finely diced
juice of ½ lemon

To serve

1 small tin of caviar
1 x 1.5 oz (40 g) bag of Lay's classic potato chips,
   crushed
1 handful of wild onion blossoms
1 handful of wild mustard blossoms

When I first started Treehouse, most of the ingredients I sourced were from the farmers' markets or round the area. I didn't have a car for a while, so I would ride around with two backpacks filled with product on my old-school bike. I first met Michael Passmore – who now provides some of the best chefs in the nation with fish and custom caviars – when he was selling live sturgeon at the farmers' market. He'd pull one out of the tank, whack it on the head and put it in a bag for me. One time I was riding home and I felt something flopping around in my backpack. I had to pull over onto the side of the road and hit that fish with a butternut squash.

Sturgeon always took the form of some sour cream and onion dish. A lot of times I'd smoke cured sturgeon chunks in a makeshift smoker made from a bamboo steamer an inch away from completely catching on fire on top of the stove. Sometimes I'd poach the sturgeon in an infused milk and every once in a while, it would be infused with spruce or redwood. This dish came about back in the days of foams, and this one definitely had an oniony 'froth', but I've decided to leave it out here.

Preheat the oven to 125°F (50°C) and line a baking tray with baking paper.
   Arrange the onion slices on the prepared tray so they're not overlapping, transfer to the oven and leave for 6–8 hours, or until completely dried out. Add them to a spice grinder with a pinch of salt and grind to a powder. Set aside.
   Add the milk, garlic, leek, bay, thyme and peppercorns to a wide saucepan. Bring to a simmer over a medium heat and continue to simmer for 5 minutes, then gently slide the chilled sturgeon fillets in and leave to poach for 8–10 minutes, or until cooked through and beginning to flake. Remove the fish from the poaching liquid and transfer to a dish, then spoon over a little of the poaching liquid and leave to cool (this will help it retain moisture as it does).
   Once cool, transfer the poached fish pieces to a mixing bowl together with the crème fraîche, chives, lemon juice and a pinch of salt. Using a spoon, break up the sturgeon and mix it together with the rest of the ingredients, checking and adjusting the seasoning as necessary.
   To serve, spoon the sturgeon mix into small round piles, garnish with dollops of caviar, the crushed potato chips and wild blossoms and sift a light dusting of the onion powder over the entire dish to finish.

Elderberry syrup

Makes approx. 6 cups/1.5 litres/51 fl oz

3 lb (1.35 kg) elderberries
4 cups (880 g/1lb 15 oz) granulated sugar

Besides dandelion greens, elderberries are probably the most common of the wild foods found in Sacramento. Elder trees grow all along the river and are super easy to spot – if you've been in the area you'll have seen one for sure. Even if you didn't recognize it. In the spring the trees are covered in huge white blossoms that I will also take home and use for cordials, creams or other dishes.

So many treehouse dinners featured elderberries in different forms. It would generally start with making an elderberry sauce. This got transformed into savory sauces, sweet sauces… There are a lot of different desserts that feature this elderberry sauce. From cheesecakes to flans, to creamy dishes, tarts with elderberries in them, even a cereal milk panacotta with elderberry which was a bit of a Sacramento nod to the chef Christina Tosi.

Picking and gathering elderberries in the summer was one of my favorite pastimes because it's always by the river, as elder trees like to grow in well-irrigated areas. So I was able to pick elderberries until I was hot and exhausted and then go and sit in the river for a little bit, or go and hit the rope swing.

To destem the elderberries (important, as they can be toxic), place them in a large ziplock bags and freeze overnight, then shake the berries off the stems the next day. Place the destemmed berries in a large bowl, cover with water and remove any leaves, twigs or stems that come to the surface. Using a large sieve, remove the cleaned berries from the bowl and transfer to a large saucepan.

Using a potato masher, lightly mash the berries over a medium heat until they begin to bubble up to a boil. Continue to mash the berries over the heat, or pulse the mixture lightly with an immersion blender, until the berries are fully broken down, then pass the mix through a chinois or fine-mesh strainer into a bowl, using the back of a ladle to extract as much liquid from the pulp as possible.

Transfer the strained elderberry liquid to a clean saucepan, add the sugar and bring to a boil, then reduce the heat to a simmer and cook down until thick and syrupy in consistency. To finish, pass the syrup through a chinois or fine-mesh strainer one more time to remove any impurities before using on pancakes, in cocktails, or on cakes, ice creams and creamy desserts like cheesecake and panna cotta.

Fried lamb necks

Serves 4

4 lb (1.8 kg) lamb necks
1 pig's trotter, split lengthways
kosher salt and freshly cracked black pepper
¼ cup (60 ml/2 fl oz) extra-virgin olive oil
2 celery stalks, diced
2 carrots, diced
1 small onion, diced
1 garlic bulb, halved widthways
1 bunch of thyme
1 rosemary sprig
2 bay leaves
1 cup (250 ml/8½ fl oz) red wine
4 cups (1 litre/34 fl oz) lamb or beef stock
½ cup (15 g/½ oz) chopped flat-leaf parsley
1 cup (60 g/2 oz) panko breadcrumbs, blitzed
   to a fine powder in a food processor
4 eggs, beaten
1 cup (150 g/5½ oz) all-purpose (plain) flour

When I first made this we jokingly called it the Borg cube of lamb because the first iteration of it, which I had rolled in chamomile breadcrumbs and fried, came out as this perfect cube on the plate. (In the end the shape, despite being perfect, felt a little weird to eat, I thought, so we moved it into a rectangle.) It's a dish that came about from my knowledge of how to make terrines and *en presse*, using the gelatin of the trotter to set everything and then cutting it into portions before breading them and frying them so that when you cut into the croquette the warm meat juices just kind of ooze out of it.

I used to serve it with this salad which was kind of stealing from this chef that I was working with at the time – he'd made this soft shell crab dish that was coming out of my station and it had this salad of snow peas and snap peas and a few other things. Ramps were in season at the time too, as it was spring, so I decided to pickle them, chop them and fold them into an aïoli, and so that's kind of how this dish came together. It stuck around on the Treehouse menu for a bit, until I eventually got tired of serving Borg cubes and rectangles.

Preheat the oven to 325°F (160°C). Line a terrine dish or loaf tin with baking paper and season the lamb necks and pig's trotter heavily with salt.
   Pour enough olive oil into a stockpot to cover the base and place it over medium–high heat. Add the lamb necks and trotter halves to the pan and sear until browned on all sides, then remove from the pan and set aside in a braising dish. Remove the excess fat from the pot, add a fresh drizzle of olive oil together with the celery, carrot, onion and garlic and cook for a few minutes, stirring occasionally, until softened. Add the thyme, rosemary and bay leaves, pour over the red wine and simmer, stirring to deglaze the pan, until reduced by half. Pour in the stock and bring to a boil, then spoon the mixture into the braising dish over seared meat pieces. Cover with baking paper, place a lid or a layer of tight-fitting foil over the top and cook in the oven for 2 hours, turning the meat pieces over halfway through cooking, until fork tender. Remove from the oven and leave everything to cool slightly in the braising liquid.
   Once cool enough to handle, pick the meat from the bones with your hands, discarding the bones and sinew. Pour the braising liquid into a small saucepan, bring to a simmer and cook for 20 minutes, or until reduced by a third. Add all of the de-boned meat to a mixing bowl

and toss with a pinch of salt, a few cracks of pepper and the chopped parsley. Press the meat mixture into the prepared terrine dish or loaf tin, pressing down on it with another similar dish or tin to really compress the meat. Ladle just enough of the reduced braising liquid over the top of meat to saturate but not completely cover it and refrigerate for 2 hours or overnight. (At this point the meat should now be one solid mass thanks to the high amount of gelatin in the trotter.)

Preheat the oven to 250°F (160°C). Blitz the panko breadcrumbs to a fine powder in a food processor and transfer to a shallow bowl. Add the beaten egg to a second shallow bowl and the flour to a third.

Carefully turn the block of meat out onto a cutting board and slice it into perfect rectangular portions. Dust the lamb pieces first in the flour bowl, then dip them in the egg and finally add them to the panko to ensure they are coated well on both sides

Heat a heavy drizzle of olive oil in a large frying pan over medium–high heat. Working in batches, fry the coated portions in the pan until golden on all sides (about 3–4 minutes per side) then finish in the oven to make sure they are warmed through. Plate and serve with a salad of of your choice.

04|12|2010

I could fuck everything up in a day.

It makes me nervous, but, really, if I wanted to ruin everything it would only take a day to do it.

It'd be easy.

It's way easier to screw everything up than it is to do good, you know?

But sometimes you just want to say, '██████ and let everything crumble. You know what I mean?

Someone was having a tough day

4. [San Francisco]

It's funny how dreams change. You long to leave home, leave your town and make your mark, but after Blackbird and Treehouse and all that shit, the time I worked in San Francisco – at Saison and at Coi – was probably the most trying time of my career. It was pretty difficult.

I wasn't living in San Francisco, really. Well, I was, but only during the weeks and I would come home on the weekends. I would take the Megabus in early – this tall, double decker bus that heads from Sacramento to San Francisco and is filled with every kind of person you can imagine, from people in suits looking like they're gearing up for something important, to younger people heading to the city just to have fun for the day. You can tell that a lot of the people on that bus were nervous, getting ready to, you know, sell themselves. Heading down for an interview, or in a transitional period in their life.

I totally was. After coming back from burning out working at Blackbird, I had landed something super amazing, something that had been the dream for so long – these Michelin-starred restaurants. Two, three Michelin-starred spots with these amazing, world-renowned chefs on the world's best list… yadda, yadda, yadda.

That was my dream. That was my dream for my entire life. But it chewed me up and spat me out. I flopped. I walked out of Saison. I took the Megabus down one Tuesday morning and I didn't go in. I had a ticket and I came back that night. My knives were in the restaurant. My clogs were in the locker. I was that terrified to go back in.

I couldn't do it anymore. I don't know why, I can't pin it on one thing. It was extremely cutthroat… I wasn't happy… and it was really hard.

I used to get on that bus at 6am on a Tuesday to go down to San Francisco – say I had Sunday, Monday off, I'd get on the bus at 6am on a Tuesday and take the bus down for two hours, get off at the spot which was close to Saison and hang out at a coffee shop and then get to work at eleven or noon, then after dinner service, get off at one in the morning. Go crash in a hostel. Then not sleep, because it was a party hostel above a strip club.

Not eating well, not sleeping well, no-one to confide in – it wasn't a good time.

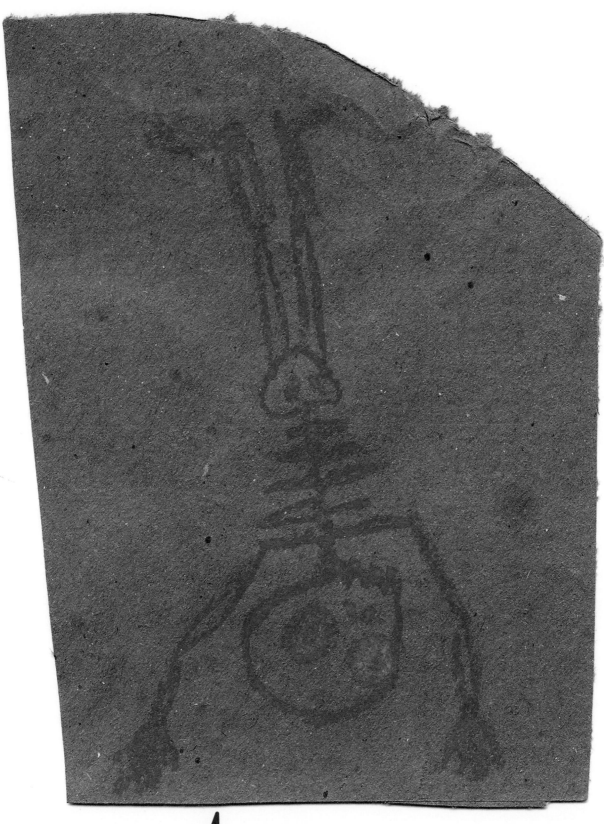

Accurate

Hoshigakiii

Anyway, one morning I got into that coffee shop, ate a grilled cheese and made the decision to walk out of Saison. It was a very, very important grilled cheese.

Why, exactly? Well, that grilled cheese was delicious. Essentially it was just bread and cheese put together, served to me on a piece of fucking wax paper, but it kind of just spilled this thought. I bit into it and the bread was toasted perfectly and the cheese had that pull that you want on a grilled cheese – it was so good and so satisfying. I don't know if it was because I was malnourished or whatever, but it was one of the best things I had eaten in a long time, which is funny to say given I was working in one of the best restaurants in the world and tasting the food there all day.

At that point, I remember thinking, 'Why is this three-Michelin-starred restaurant better than this grilled cheese? And are the things that make it better worth being unhappy for?'

And they just weren't, to me.

Apart from talking it through with a friend on the phone, though, I didn't tell anybody about it for a long time. I pretended to go to San Francisco for a week to my family. They were so supportive and, obviously, getting everything I needed to get down to the restaurant wasn't free. You know, I don't know why I wasn't just like, 'Hey, I'm sorry you guys I tried but this isn't for me'. It was one of the most embarrassing, demeaning, humiliating, just fucking straight-up kick in the nuts that I've ever given myself. Your lifelong dream is to work in one of the world's best restaurants and you finally do and you're getting there and you see the path that you can take to achieve the dream that you created as a boy and… you don't want anything to do with it. I don't know, for a long time I was almost in denial. I made up stories, I just… said things how they weren't actually and it took me a long time to come to terms with it.

Chasing Harvest

Hit the road

3/20/19

Yesterday, I took the Megabus back down to San Francisco. I went to check out this awesome building where we are going to have this rad party. It had this incredible view of the city – you walk out onto this terrace with this pool and firepits and all these trees with this amazing panoramic view.

The day's going great. I've got my skateboard, I've been to Bluestone Lane cafe where I've gotten a Vegemite toast and a flat white, closed my eyes and pretended I was back in Melbourne for a moment. It's even been sunny in the city, which never really happens. I've just visited the Ferry Building, which is now a small farmers' market and smelled some wild mushrooms, I've even hung out by the water s̶~~ ~~ and listened to some reggae, kind of fucking around and giving myself an hour or two break before heading home because I haven't really had time off – or time out of Sacramento – for such a long time. Anyway, after all that I've gone and put the bus stop in my GPS to skate back to it and head home and end up skating right past Saison. All the doors are open and they are getting kitchen deliveries. I slow down on my skateboard and peer into the kitchen.

It's just, really… I guess I experienced something like PTSD. You know, I start sweating. I get this nervous feeling in my gut. And then I look at all the cooks. I don't recognize anybody because they're all new cooks there because the turnover is insane. And I look in and every one of them is doing what so many people view as the best work in the world. You know, they're ranked as one of the best restaurants in the world, so these cooks are some of the best cooks in the world. But as I kind of get over this shaky, uneasy feeling I simultaneously felt pity, jealousy, and just, like, support for these guys. Like, keep doing it, that kind of thing. You know you're working really fucking hard, so good on you.

It was kind of the closure I needed, that whole thing. And I didn't realize that I needed it until I skated by there and realized that this was physically affecting me. But as I thought about it I was like, 'Kevin, you know you didn't just walk out, right? You left everything there. You left your coats. You left your knife bag and roll. You left your clogs. You left your dreams. You left your…' Well, at the time I was leaving my career.

I left the support that my family was giving me through all of this. I left the encouragement of my friends telling me that I was going to be the next greatest chef and that this was so cool, you know, 'Look at my friend Kevin – we're going to miss you when you're in San Francisco but we're going to support you with a going away party and all this shit'. I left it all there in that locker in Saison to just get thrown away. I think I called someone back a month after I left, when I'd finally worked up enough courage to ask someone whether my stuff was there and they were like, 'No, it's not. Good day.'

So, yeah, that was yesterday. It was pretty wild.

Velvet Underground Pale Blue eyes

5. [Cobram]

Even after Saison, Michelin stars were still the dream, even after I shattered it. It was, 'Well, where do I go from here? How do I still achieve that dream? Maybe I should go back to Sacramento, open another restaurant…?'

So I did. Well, I started to. Until ~~XXXXX~~ jumped ship to Australia.

At the time I was working at Saddlerock, the name of the restaurant that I was opening, when I got the gig to do the food for Cobram's first harvest lunch in California. Saddlerock was the name of the first restaurant that was an institution in Sacramento and we were recycling some of the branding and the name itself – playing off this goldrush vibe.

Anyway, I was in the Saddlerock kitchen getting prepped for the lunch for Cobram the night before, trying to figure out what I was going to make for dessert. I had the rest of the menu pretty much sorted out and prepped but I always push pastry and dessert back to last. Always. Often it's me just procrastinating, because it's not really my strength.

So, there were all these beautiful Nantes carrots – really good carroty carrots, like Bugs Bunny carrots – that were coming out of a nearby farm. Job done, I thought – I'll probably just do a carrot cake and it could be cool if I used olive oil in the batter. Easy. Then I thought about looking at what else was around as well as ways to incorporate them. Persimmons were looking pretty rad, maybe I could give them a brunoise and put them in some honey or something?

At this stage I was still really overthinking dishes rather than doing simple, good stuff on a plate. I started thinking about other elements too and instead of doing a typical cream cheese frosting on top, I started toying with the idea of doing a buttercream frosting or something like that instead. At that point it was 11 o'clock at night and I'd been working all day, so I pulled out a few cubes of butter to get soft and, given I didn't have much else left to do until it did, I went to the bar across the street for a whiskey while I waited. I sat down, ordered my drink and Tim the barman was talking to me but I just couldn't get that cake out of my head. All I was thinking was, 'Why the hell am I topping that thing with butter as a last bite for a first olive harvest lunch? Do you think those guys are going to talk shit if I serve them buttercream frosting? Really?'.

That's when I had the thought. 'Olive oil's a fat, same as butter... why don't I just put olive oil and icing sugar together?' I left the bar, went back into the kitchen, took down a bottle of extra virgin and some icing sugar, put them into a KitchenAid and produced the most awesome icing I've ever tasted. With just two ingredients.

I suppose the rest is history. The cake, along with the rest of the meal, was a huge hit, and a few days later I got the call from Dan that changed my life.

It was hard. At the time, I thought I had already fallen in love with food again. I thought I was re-inspired. But, really, I was just replicating this shit that I've done in all those restaurants before. I'd been doing a ton of research and figuring out Sacramento food and what inspired Sacramento's food scene, blah, blah blah, all this stuff that chefs say. You know, their region – which is great – but I still wasn't ready. And it wasn't right. I wasn't cooking with my heart.

KEVIN O'CONNOR
Executive Chef

SADDLE ROCK

1801 L St. Sacramento

chefkevinoconnor@gmail.com   Cell: 916-254-1799
saddlerockresturaunt.com Reservations: 916-443-1010

Worst Cards I've ever had

Truth be told, I wasn't even ready when I started with Cobram. I didn't realize at the time what we would end up doing. I didn't know that it would be a case of, 'Ok, quit your job at the restaurant and you're going to travel the world, you're going to write a book and you're going to have all these awesome opportunities to cook in other places in the world and fucking whatever'. I didn't know. I had no idea what I was going to do. I knew I was going to be cooking in Australia, but beyond that, I had no ~~fucking~~ idea.

But my relationship, my home life and my work life were, it felt at the time, parallel in their downhill descent. And I saw a way to just get out. To hop out of the plane, to pull the parachute and float away.

Sometimes you've just got to go away to really come home.

True Aussie cook-out on the banks of the Murray

Vegemite and coffee-braised boar shoulder

Serves 8

1 × boar shoulder or pork shoulder
  (approx. 5 lb/2.25 kg), bone in
kosher salt
¼ cup (20 g/¾ oz) ground coffee
2 tablespoons Vegemite
2 tablespoons extra-virgin olive oil, plus extra
  for drizzling
1 onion, diced
2 celery stalks, diced
1 carrot, diced
1 garlic bulb, halved widthways
1 bunch of thyme
2 bay leaves
1 × 12 fl oz (350 ml) bottle of cola
8 cups (2 litres/68 fl oz) beef or chicken stock,
  heated until boiling

To serve (optional)

Mole Californio (see page 42)
sliced radishes
pickled leeks or red onions
fresh herbs
smashed avocado

When I first made this I knew I wanted to bring in an Aussie element, because I was cooking for Americans and we were using both American and Australian oils and I wanted to highlight the fact that we are Australian. When I first tasted Vegemite I really didn't like it but after two or three years of being exposed to it, I'm now a full-blown Vegemite fiend. For those first couple of years though I tended to use it more as an ingredient (rather than spread on toast) as in this dish here, which combines Vegemite, ground coffee and olive oil to make a super umami-rich rub that is slathered over the boar shoulder to add an extra layer of depth and richness to the meat before it is roasted over the fire.

Salt the boar shoulder generously all over with kosher salt. Mix the coffee, Vegemite and olive oil together in a small bowl to form a paste-like rub. Spread the rub evenly over the shoulder and leave to rest for 15–20 minutes.

Place a grill grate about 8 in (20 cm) above hot, glowing coals, or heat your grill (barbecue) to medium–high heat. Preheat the oven to 325°F (160°C).

Cook the boar shoulder over the fire, turning occasionally, until all sides are evenly caramelized.

Meanwhile, add the onion, celery, carrot, garlic and herbs to a medium saucepan along with a drizzle of olive oil and cook, stirring, until just beginning to colour. Add the cola and beef stock, bring to a simmer and leave for 10–15 minutes to thicken and reduce slightly.

Transfer the shoulder from the grill to a braising dish. Pour over the braising liquid, then cover everything firstly with a sheet of baking paper and then with a lid or a sheet of tight-fitting foil. Cook in the oven for 2½–3 hours, or until a knife can be inserted into the meat without any effort.

Leave the meat to cool slightly in the braising liquid, then divide it among plates. Serve with my Mole Californio and some bright accompaniments like sliced radishes, pickled leeks or red onions, fresh herbs and smashed avocado, if you like.

Carrot cake FFS

Serves 16–18

3 large eggs, at room temperature
2 cups (440 g/15½ oz) sugar
⅓ cup (80 ml/2½ fl oz) nonfat buttermilk,
  at room temperature
1 lb (450 g) carrots, peeled and finely grated
1½ cups (375 ml/12½ fl oz) extra-virgin olive oil,
  plus extra for drizzling
3 cups (450 g/1 lb) all-purpose (plain) flour,
  plus extra for dusting
2 teaspoons baking powder
1 teaspoon baking soda (bicarbonate of soda)
1 teaspoon salt
finely sliced carrot ribbons or carrot tops, to serve
  (optional)

Buttercream

¾ cup (90 g/3 oz) confectioners' (icing) sugar
6 tablespoons (90 ml/3 fl oz) extra-virgin olive oil

As I write this it's approaching US harvest and I'm about to make my first carrot cake of the year (Hazel has stepped up to the task in the past, but I'm not ready to palm this one off on her just yet!). There are a lot of nostalgic smells that kind of bring back the idea of harvest. There are a lot of people who are around during harvest and there are a lot of feelings and memories and excitement for this time, but nothing compares to a taste of this carrot cake batter to bring me back to those many different harvests because it has been such a staple. That first year I made it I didn't actually taste the cake and frosting together at all until after I served it – I remember people at that lunch eating it and losing their shit over it and I thought they were just drunk by that point and stoked to have cake, but then I tasted it and realized how incredibly well those two elements worked together. We joke about it being the cake that got me my job, and I suppose that's not far from the truth.

Preheat the oven to 325°F (160°C).

Grease a large 9 × 13 in (23 × 34 cm) cake tin or two 8 in (20 cm) round cake tin with a drizzle of olive oil. Dust with flour and tap out any excess. Set aside.

Whisk together the eggs and sugar in a large bowl until pale and creamy. Whisk in the buttermilk, carrots and olive oil. In a separate medium bowl, whisk together the flour, baking powder, baking soda and salt. Stir the flour mixture into the carrot mixture until completely combined, then transfer the batter to the prepared tin or tins and bake for 1 hour 15 minutes, or until a cake tester inserted in the center comes out clean.

While the cake is baking, prepare the buttercream by thoroughly and vigorously whisking the confectioners' sugar and olive oil together.

Unmold the cake onto a cooling rack and leave it to cool completely before spreading the buttercream over the top. Decorate with carrot ribbons or cleaned carrot tops, if you like.

'Taste does not come by chance: it is a long,
laborious task to acquire it.'

Chapter 2

Away

Australian Harvest.

It's a few days until harvest and I'm excited to be heading back out to Australia.

I feel like you can't compare Australia Harvest to California Harvest because it's so different. We don't have people with us in Oz for a few days because they're already familiar with who we are and what we do, whereas in California we really have to show them everything – not just how we produce oil, the health benefits, the lab and all that, but also how we act, how we talk, how we have fun, how we eat and how we let loose, you know.

I'm in the middle of nowhere in Australia. But I'm able to focus solely on what I'm supposed to do there, precisely because of that. I'm not on a computer. I'm not dealing with other shit. I'm not worrying about what people are coming and what our impact is going to be, and it's not one big shot that we can't fuck up. It's just cook and do your thing and kill it. Every. Single. Day. It's the wildest place I've ever cooked, probably, but it has so many elements that are similar to cooking in a professional kitchen. There's extremes of weather. You know shit's going to break and you can't get it fixed in time. You've got people coming at a fixed time each day. You know the door's open at a certain time every single day, no matter what.

And you just gotta go fast.

Vintage Mining Cart, turned
Argentinian BBQ

Neil Young- Harvest Moon

I almost like the food I make more in Australia because every day I'm shooting from the hip and it's kind of against all odds with the timing, because you're getting a different group in every single day.

In California I have everything at my fingertips – ingredients, set-up, the lot. I have the menu down three days prior to an event and everything's ordered. But in Australia I'm limited to a spectrum and I'm able to flourish within that. That limited availability and the difficulties seem to combine to create something even more interesting.

You have to get more creative when you're limited like that. And not just limited by the ingredients that are available, but also the knowledge of them, the timing and just the sheer difficulty of cooking for up to 30 people a day by yourself. In California I've got so much support – farmers, friends, people in the company, even down to my mom being there.

But I'm able to schedule things a little better in Australia. I know I've gotta start my fire at 6:30 to have a coal bed, so I can start braising the short ribs in the camp oven so they're done by this time. And I'm able to just cook, serve, clean up, prep some more... have a wine, make some dinner, prep some more, finish dinner, go to bed, wake up, start three fires and continue doing that for 60 days or so.

Chapa bread

Serves 12

3 cups (450 g/1 lb) all-purpose (plain) or bread flour
1 cup (100 g/3½ oz) spelt flour, plus extra for dusting
2¼ teaspoons active dry yeast
1 tablespoon salt, plus extra to serve
1 tablespoon extra-virgin olive oil, plus extra to serve
1½–2 cups (375–500 ml/12½–17 fl oz) warm water

This is an adaptation of a recipe by Francis Mallmann, an Argentine chef who has been a huge influence on me. I remember when I was working at Ella when I was 20 or 21 and I was into Michelin stars and molecular gastronomy (that's when that was popping off) and my mentor there was telling me that I shouldn't focus on all these trends, that the pendulum was starting to swing in the other direction and that simplicity was cool, too. I didn't listen to him, of course, because I was 21, but he had some serious foresight. These days I like to greet everybody at the shack with this warm bread and it feels like this is kind of an ode to that return to simplicity, I guess.

I use a locally milled spelt flour in the dough which just tastes phenomenal, so when people come into the shack, sit down and pour their wines, everybody's welcomed, and this is generally the first bite. I welcome everybody to break the bread together and dip it into some ridiculously fresh olive oil.

In a large bowl, mix the flours, yeast, and salt together with a whisk. Gradually add the olive oil and the warm water, stirring with a wooden spoon, until a sticky dough forms. Work the dough together a little bit with your hands – sprinkling in a little more flour if the dough is wet and really sticky or adding a splash of water if it's dense and hard to work with – then leave to sit and relax for 5 minutes before kneading it until it's soft and pliable. Chuck the kneaded dough into a bowl drizzled with a little olive oil, cover it with a damp towel and leave it to rise in a warm place for 1 hour (near to the fire is good for this, just be careful not to put it too close or you run the risk of cooking it).

Lightly dust a clean surface or big cutting board with a little extra spelt flour, tip out the risen dough and roll it out to a rough ¼ in (5 mm thick) rectangle. Cut the dough into rough 3–4 in (7.5–10 cm) squares, then transfer the squares to a dusted tray and cover again with a damp tea towel. Leave to prove for another 30 minutes.

Place a plancha (hotplate) about 12 in (30 cm) above hot, glowing coals, or on top of a grill (barbecue) at medium heat. Place the chapa squares on the plancha and cook for 5 minutes, turning halfway through cooking, or until golden brown on each side. Quickly brush each side with olive oil (I like to use some fresh rosemary or thyme trimmings from the garden as the brush here to give it a little more flavour), then sprinkle over salt and eat immediately with extra olive oil for dipping.

Twice-cooked beets, herbed yogurt, crisped barley

Serves 10–12

6–8 medium beets, peeled
sea salt
1 teaspoon coriander seeds
1 teaspoon white peppercorns
2 bay leaves
2 oranges or mandarins, 1 whole, 1 halved
1 cup (220 g/8 oz) pearled barley
3 cups (750 ml/25½ fl oz) water
1 cup (250 g/9 oz) plain Greek yogurt
¼ cup (15 g/½ oz) roughly chopped herbs
   (such as mint, parsley, oregano, chives),
   plus extra to serve
¼ cup (60 ml/2 fl oz) extra-virgin olive oil,
   plus extra for drizzling

I've got this beautiful plancha that sits over the fire in the shack, and one day I decided I'd marinate some beets in olive oil and cook them up a bit on it; there's so much sugar in beets that they caramelize up nicely and create this whole extra layer of charred, sweet, cotton candy-like flavor. I treated the barley the same way – just tossing it in oil and laying it down on the plancha until I almost forgot about it to give it this nice crispiness – and the yogurt helps add those creamy, herbaceous notes to the dish that the charred and crispy elements are kind of missing.

Toss the beets in a drizzle of olive oil, season liberally with salt, then transfer to a roasting dish and scatter over the spices and bay leaves. Cut the whole orange into ½ in (1 cm) pieces and arrange these around the beets, then pour over enough water to fill the dish to a depth of ½ in (1 cm). Cover the dish with a layer of baking paper and then a tight layer of foil, transfer to the oven and roast for 40–50 minutes, or until a sharp knife inserted into the center of one of the beets comes out easily. Remove from the oven and leave to cool slightly, then rub off the skins (a dish towel will help here).

In a medium saucepan, cover the pearled barley with the water. With a lid on, simmer for approximately 45 minutes, or until barley is tender, but still has some chew. Strain off any excess liquid, then let the barley steam, off the heat with the lid on, for 5–10 minutes. Set aside until needed.

Mix the yogurt, chopped herbs, 2 tablespoons of olive oil and a pinch of salt together in a bowl, add the cooled beets and mix again well. Set aside in the fridge for 1 hour, or overnight, to allow the flavors to develop.

Place a plancha (hotplate) about 6 in (15 cm) above hot, glowing coals, or on top of a grill (barbecue) at high heat.

Remove one of the beets from the bowl and, using the base of your palm, smash it into halves or thirds, however it breaks up (if you have kitchen gloves then wear them as this will stain your hands if not). Repeat with the remaining beets, setting aside the herbed yogurt for later use. Toss the smashed beets in another 2 tablespoons of olive oil and season with salt, then transfer to the plancha and cook for about 3 minutes on each side, or until caramelized all over. Squeeze over the juice from the orange halves and continue to cook until the juice has bubbled and evaporated and the beets are glazed, then remove the beets from the heat and set aside to cool slightly.

Toss the cooked barley in a generous drizzle of olive oil, then transfer to the plancha and spread out in a thin, even layer. Leave to toast for 3–4 minutes, or until nicely brown and crispy, then transfer to a serving bowl and season to taste. Top with the beets, dolllop over the herbed yogurt and scatter over a few extra herb leaves to finish.

Fire-dried tomatoes

Makes as many as you like

roma tomatoes
fresh extra-virgin olive oil
salt
a red gum fire, or any hardwood fire

These are another one of those things that have come about because of my wanting to use the fire as much as I can. Apart from wood costing money, the fire is something that is constantly emitting flavor opportunities until it dies. So, with an abundance of tomatoes around me, I just decided to start cutting them and tossing them in olive oil and putting them on racks and dehydrating them over the fire.

I'd raise the racks almost as high as they could go, and after six hours or so they would be almost like sun-dried tomatoes. I'd then pack them and preserve them in picual oil, which tastes a lot like tomatoes, and the pairing is just really lovely and it's something great to have in the fridge at a pinch, especially when you've got surprise guests at the shack and you need to whip up something like the polenta, poached egg and tomato dish opposite.

Cut the tomatoes in half lengthways and remove any remnants of stem. Toss the tomato halves in a generous drizzle of fresh olive oil and a few pinches of salt to coat evenly, then transfer, cut side down, to a wire rack. Place the wire rack over the fire at a height that will allow them to roast slowly, adding a few fresh logs to provide some extra smoke, and roast for up to 2 hours, carefully turning occasionally with tongs, until the tomatoes are caramelized and significantly wrinkled.

Remove the roasted tomatoes from the rack and spoon into screw-top jars, then pour over enough fresh olive oil to cover and transfer to the fridge until needed. (So long as they are completely covered by the oil the tomatoes will keep for weeks.)

Creamy white polenta, preserved fire tomatoes, soft eggs

Serves 8

2 cups (500 ml/17 fl oz) whole (full-cream) milk
1½ cups (375 ml/12½ fl oz) water
½ teaspoon sea salt
¾ cup (110 g/4 oz) stone-ground white polenta
¼ cup (60 ml/2 fl oz) extra-virgin olive oil

To serve

8 poached eggs
14–16 Fire-dried Tomatoes (see opposite), warmed
1 handful of roughly torn herbs (such as oregano,
   thyme and marjoram)
sea salt flakes
extra-virgin olive oil

This happened on one of my days off, when I was hit with a few surprise guests who came for a visit to Cobram Estate. I, of course, wanted to treat them for lunch but didn't really have much going on in the kitchen, so I shot from the hip. I found a few jars of these olive oil-preserved tomatoes and some dried polenta in the pantry, and along with some eggs and herbs from the property that was pretty much all that was needed. The whole thing came together naturally and was very well received.

Add the milk, water and salt to a saucepan and bring to a boil. Slowly sprinkle the polenta into the pan, whisking vigorously as you go to incorporate, and continue to cook, whisking, until slightly thickened and showing signs of spitting or bubbling. Reduce the heat to low, cover with a lid and cook for 30–40 minutes, whisking and scraping down the sides of the pan every 5 minutes or so, until the polenta starts to pull away from the sides. Remove from the heat, whisk in the olive oil and season to taste.

Spoon the creamy polenta into a serving bowl, pressing down on it with the back of a spoon to make small indentations for the poached eggs. Serve topped with the poached eggs, warmed tomatoes, a scattering of roughly torn herbs, a little flaky salt and a victory drizzle of olive oil.

Fire-roasted grapes

Makes as many as you like

whole clusters of red, seedless grapes
extra-virgin olive oil, for drizzling
salt

During my very first year out in Australia, back before there was a shack, there was absolutely nothing – it was pretty much just a clearing in an olive grove with a fire on the ground, some basic cookware and a tiny shack which we now use as a generator shed with maybe six feet (2 meters) of bench space to use. And I was happy as a clam.

Anyway, on that first drive up to Boundary Bend I really took my time getting up there, collecting a lot of produce from the little roadside stands as I went, and one of the things I bought was a whole box of grapes. I wasn't sure what I was going to do with them (though I knew if I didn't do anything with them, well, at least I liked eating grapes) but on the first day before the guests came I was prepping and experimenting a little bit and I dumped a dozen or so clusters of grapes onto the hot coals. After they'd blistered a bit and charred I picked them up and lightly dusted off the ash and, well, it was unlike anything I'd had before. I'd roasted grapes in the oven but this was quite different – they had a definite scorched side that was super charred and black but the other side still had this fresh pop of juicy fresh grape, giving you this beautiful contrast and a super unique flavor.

Toss the grapes in a large mixing bowl with a drizzle of olive oil and a sprinkle of salt. Place the grapes on a hot grill (barbecue) or directly onto the hot coals of a fire and cook, turning once or twice, until the majority of the grapes are scorched and nicely caramelized. Remove from the heat and enjoy simply as they are, as part of my beef cheek recipe (see opposite) or made into a special hoisin sauce (see page 130).

Braised beef cheeks with fire-roasted grapes and grilled onions

Serves 8

4 beef cheeks, trimmed and cleaned
kosher salt
extra-virgin olive oil
1 celery stalk, chopped
1 carrot, chopped
1 onion, chopped
1 garlic bulb, halved widthways
2 bay leaves
2 thyme sprigs
2 rosemary sprigs
1 teaspoon black peppercorns
2 cups (500 ml/17 fl oz) red wine
2 cups (500 ml/17 fl oz) beef or chicken stock
2 medium clusters of Fire-roasted Grapes
  (see opposite), to serve

Grilled onions

3 small red onions
extra-virgin olive oil
salt
a splash of red wine vinegar

These beef cheeks are really hard to screw up. I love that you can chuck this in a camp oven, bury it in a fire and get back to it four hours later and it'll end up as a beautifully glazed, falling apart, meaty, melty gift like this. The richness of the braise is perfect with the sweet pop of the caramelized grapes, while the grilled onions help to bring the two elements together and cuts right through that fattiness as well.

Preheat the oven to 325°F (160°C) oven or get a fire suitable for cooking going. Season the beef cheeks generously with kosher salt all over.

Warm a few glugs of olive oil in a Dutch oven (casserole dish) set over a high heat. Add the beef cheeks and sear until nicely browned on all sides. Setting the meat aside, lower the heat to medium, add the celery, carrot, onion, garlic, bay leaves, herbs and peppercorns to the Dutch oven and cook, stirring occasionally, until the veg begins to color.

Pour over the red wine, bring to a boil and cook, scraping the bottom of the dish with a wooden spoon as you go, until the liquid has reduced by about a quarter. Add the stock and return to a simmer, then lower in the beef cheeks, pressing down on them with a spoon to make sure they are at least half submerged in the liquid. Spread a layer of baking paper over the dish, cover with the lid and transfer to the preheated oven – or set next to the fire's embers placing a few coals on top – and cook for 3 hours, turning the beef cheeks after 1 hour, or until the meat is tender and the liquid has reduced down to a glaze-like consistency. Set aside, covered, to cool for 1 hour.

While the beef is cooling, cook the red onions. Fire up your grill (barbecue) and get it nice and hot. Cut the red onions into quarters from top to bottom, leaving the skin, bases and everything intact. Toss the onions in olive oil and sprinkle with salt, then transfer to the grill and cook, turning, until charred on all sides. Transfer the onions to a bowl together with red wine vinegar and toss together, then cover the bowl tightly with plastic wrap. Leave the onions to sit and steam for at least 30 minutes before removing and discarding the onion skins and bases with a sharp knife. Set aside the onion flesh

Once cooled, remove the beef cheeks from the braise and slice them into large, manageable chunks. Meanwhile, return the Dutch oven to the heat and reduce the braising liquids even further until glossy. To serve, divide the red onion, beef pieces and grapes among plates, spoon over a little of the reduced braising liquid and finish everything off with a drizzle of olive oil.

Five-spice kangaroo with roast grape hoisin and crispy saltbush

Serves 8

2 kangaroo striploins
1 tablespoon extra-virgin olive oil,
  plus extra for deep-frying and drizzling
1 teaspoon salt
2 teaspoons Chinese five-spice powder
2 loosely packed cups (60 g/2 oz) saltbush leaves

Roast grape hoisin

1 tablespoon extra-virgin olive oil
1 shallot, finely sliced
1 teaspoon grated fresh ginger
½ cup (50 g/2 oz) Fire-roasted Grapes
  (see page 126), picked off the clusters,
  plus extra to serve
¼ cup (60 ml/2 fl oz) honey
2 tablespoons yellow miso paste
2 tablespoons rice wine vinegar
3 tablespoons soy sauce
1½ teaspoons cornstarch (cornflour),
  mixed together with 1½ teaspoons water

After making up that first iteration of roasted grapes (see page 126), I decided I wanted to serve them with kangaroo; it was my first trip to Oz and I was absolutely frothing to cook 'roo. I'd also been inspired by a lot of the really great Chinese and Southeast Asian food in Melbourne, so I decided to do a kangaroo bao with roasted grape hoisin, using those roasted grapes as the base for a hoisin. I served them up with a small clustering of the roasted grapes on the side to allow people to pick and graze and add them to their bao as they ate, enjoying the very best of the produce that came from around Boundary Bend.

Since then the dish has evolved a bit – I've dropped the bao and added crispy fried saltbush leaves (there's a ton of it that grows around the shack) to lend some crunch and a different textural contrast to that super tender, rare kangaroo.

Start by rubbing the kangaroo loins together with the olive oil, salt and five-spice powder in a bowl. Transfer to the fridge and leave to marinate for 1 hour.

To make the hoisin, warm the olive oil in a heavy-based saucepan, add the shallot and ginger and sauté until beautifully aromatic. Add all the remaining ingredients except the cornstarch and bring to a boil, then lower the heat to a simmer and leave to bubble away, stirring occasionally, for 5 minutes. Remove the pan from the heat, carefully pour the contents into a blender and blend together until smooth. Pass the sauce through a fine strainer back into the saucepan and return to the boil, then slowly whisk in the cornstarch mixture and cook for 1–2 minutes until thickened. Remove from the heat and set aside.

Heat a deep-fat fryer or a large, wide saucepan half-filled with olive oil to 350°F (180°C). Lower the saltbush leaves into the hot oil and fry for 1 minute or until they curl and crisp. Some larger leaves will need to be flipped. Using a slotted spoon, remove the leaves from the oil and place them on a paper towel-lined tray. Season with salt and set aside.

Place a grill grate about 6 in (15 cm) above hot, glowing coals, or heat your grill (barbecue) to high. While the grill is heating, remove the 'roo from the fridge and leave it to come to room temperature.

Lay the kangaroo on the hot grill plate and cook for 2–3 minutes on each side, or until heavily seared all over but still rare. Remove from the heat and leave to rest for 5 minutes.

While the 'roo is resting, spread a thin layer of the hoisin across a large serving platter. Thinly slice the 'roo and arrange the pieces around the platter in one layer. Drizzle over some oil, sprinkle over some flaky salt and scatter over the crispy saltbush leaves and some extra roasted grapes to finish.

Fat Freddy's Drop
The Big BW

Quince mess

Serves 12

1 cup (250 ml/8½ fl oz) heavy whipping cream
2 tablespoons sugar
½ teaspoon ground wattle seeds
raw whole honeycomb, to serve (optional)

Quince

4 large or 6 medium quince
5 cups (1.25 litres/42 fl oz) water
1 cup (220 g/8 oz) sugar
1 cup (250 ml/8½ fl oz) white wine
½ cup (125 ml/4 fl oz) honey
2 tablespoons dried rosebuds
1 lemon, halved
pinch of salt

Meringue

3 large egg whites, at room temperature
pinch of salt
½ cup (110 g/4 oz) caster (superfine) sugar
¾ cup (90 g/3 oz) confectioners' (icing) sugar

A lot of my Australian dishes are the result of making do with what I have to hand, and this is definitely one of those. It came about because I reached a point where I had grown so tired of doing 'The Carrot Cake That Everyone Wanted' that I couldn't stand it anymore. So, I took the honey from the bees that pollinate the almond and orange trees that surround the grove, along with local quince and eggs, and put the lot together to make this kind of layered dessert. The first guest who tried it told me that it was a lot like an Eton mess but I had to look that up as I hadn't heard of it. (Turns out it's an actual thing).

Anyway, I still like to make this dessert. Oftentimes, I'll put rose petals and white wine into the quince poaching liquid, just to make it a little more aromatic and play off the floral notes of the honey.

Preheat the oven to 200°F (95°C). Line a baking sheet with baking paper.

For the meringue, beat the egg whites and salt together with an electric whisk until soft peaks form. Continuing to whisk, add the sugar 1 tablespoon at a time until all the sugar has been added and the meringue is stiff and glossy. Gradually fold in the confectioners' sugar until it is all incorporated, then immediately spoon the mix out onto the prepared baking sheet. Using a spatula, spread the meringue out into a rough ½ in (1 cm) thick rectangle and bake for 2–3 hours, or until the meringue is stiff and dry. Turn off the oven, crack open the door with a metal utensil and leave the meringue to cool inside it for at least 1 hour.

While the meringue is cooling, prepare the quince. Cut the tops and bottoms off the quince and peel off the skins, then place the fruit in a large saucepan or stockpot with the water, sugar, wine, honey, rosebuds, lemon halves and a pinch of salt. Bring the poaching liquid to a simmer, then cover the pan with a piece of baking paper with an 'X' cut in the center to allow steam to escape. Cook the quince for at least 1 hour, or until they are soft. Remove the quince from the poaching liquid and set aside to cool, then cut the flesh away from the cores and slice it into bite-sized pieces. Bring the poaching liquid to a boil and reduce it down to a glossy syrup, then remove from the heat and set aside until needed.

Whisk the cream and sugar together until stiff peaks form. Fold in the wattle seed.

To serve, arrange the quince pieces on a platter, leaving room for all the other components. Spoon chunks of honeycomb and dollops of whipped cream around the quince and break over pieces of the meringue by hand to fill in the empty spaces. Finish with a drizzle of the reduced poaching liquid.

A trip to the plant with Hazel...

Hey, you. You still there? Good. I've got something to show you, so come on, get in the car. It's time to go for a drive.

Nah, not back home to California, just to check out processing. And I hope we see that squirrelly little kangaroo again on the way. That little fast boy. Ah yeah, there he is! That's Spooky Boy over there.

The groves here are really big. No, scrap that, they're ~~fucking~~ massive. Endless. I always forget how huge they are and then every once in a while when I'm bombing through them I realize I've been driving for 10 or 15 minutes and I have that epiphany. This is So. Much. Fruit. It's beautiful.

It's just wild to think that we're surrounded by millions of trees and millions of stars in this little kitchen that's in the middle of nowhere – that's mostly accessed by aircraft – and creating these experiences out of this space. That's wild. And people say, 'Wow, that's fucking nuts, that's crazy' and you're like 'Yeah, you know, it's just my life'. But it is crazy to have become accustomed to looking at this sea of flickering green and silver leaves every single day. You have coffee, chop wood, look out over the trees… I'd say it's only about once a week that you're actually conscious of how many trees there are. The rest of the time you're just going through the motions, not noticing them. That's why sometimes I like to go down one of the rows of trees and just look down at them and feel, I don't know, just extremely grateful for it all.

Anyway, where was I? Oh yeah, here we are, we've arrived. These trucks are nuts, huh? There's just tanker truck after tanker truck filling up with oil, all in a line. They're making so much oil here that, for months on end, there's just always a truck in the queue to take it out of the tanks and bring it down to get bottled. It's just insane. We're so lucky.

Now, have you looked over there? See, there's more trucks over there servicing one, two, three, four pits. We've got trucks coming back here all day dumping literal truckloads of fruit. And check out the fruit on top of this giant crate – it's what the Aussies would say is 'chock-a-block', meaning completely full, chock full. Homeboy over there is using a sort of push broom to feed the fruit up into the lines that we're about to see, being careful not to puncture it as he goes. Would you look at all that fruit. It's insane.

Right, it's getting super cold out here. Let's get inside.

This is a farmstand that's about 15 minutes from my kitchen.

Colossus came to hang at the shack

So, they added a couple of extra lines this year. I remember the first time I ever came in here, I think at the time we only had two lines in California. And there's 1, 2, 3, 4, 5… 8 lines here. This is one of the biggest productions of any product I've ever seen. And it happens to be this really, really, really good shit.

It's really loud in here. Like, deafening; you can understand why people are wearing ear protection up here and why our master miller is hard of hearing these days. We'll walk through here to the hoppers – we'll have to be really careful as it's going to be slippery. Look, right through the middle here, let's take that route.

Ah, there's Herman! It's always really good to see Herman because he's so gentle and sweet (for an Argentine Viking). When you've had an interaction with him you feel that everything's all right, mainly because he doesn't speak a lot of English and he can't tell you how intense everything is, he just smiles and nods, and that's all you really want anyone to do at this point.

Now look up there, look at all that fruit dumping. It's pretty hypnotic. Watching these belts spewing out fruit and all these millions of olives building and building and building and then just cascading down when this hopper eventually fills up like all those others ones. Did you ever watch Duck Tales, where Uncle Scrooge would swim around in his gold coins? It reminds me of that. Sometimes I just want to pull an Uncle Scrooge and jump through all these olives and swim round.

So, after the trucks dump the fruit into the pits, the belts stick it up into this hopper, this hopper collects the fruit and it's gravity-fed into these discs with teeth on it, which is the mill, and it grinds it and makes this emulsion of olive – the fruit and the pit (it crushes the pit into pieces, which tears the fruit) and it creates this emulsified paste mixture. Those mills are what's so loud in here. The belts are loud but those things are just grinding and crushing this fruit day in and day out. They change the teeth depending on the ripeness, the cultivar, whatever that guy over there in the American hat says – he's in charge of a lot of the technical shit in here.

Now, come through here. This is my favorite room in the place, we call it the blue room, and there's no prizes on offer for guessing why. Anyway, after the fruit gets crushed in those mills with those teeth, it creates that paste mixture which then gets pumped into these blue malaxers, which keep that paste at a very controlled, somewhat warm temperature, and churn and break it down until, essentially, the oil is extracted from the fruit.

Here, take a look. So, when I open this little door you're going to be hit with warm olive goodness. And it's churning in there… this particular malaxer is almost empty but it's created a lot of oil tonight. And that's that paste starting to separate that emulsion. The malaxer is one of the most crucial parts of the process. It's an art. You run the machine too long, you'll get a lot of oil, but it will be over malaxed and it won't be any good – it won't make extra-virgin. You don't run it long enough and you'll probably get some really good oil, but not that much and you won't make any ███████ money. So there's a sweet spot that happens in the malaxer between how much oil you can produce and the quality of that oil. The whole setup reminds me of a kitchen. You know, you've got the lines in the mills which are like the prep cooks and the people receiving everything. The malaxer is like the badass cook who's actually cooking the shit and then it goes through to the chef and gets wiped and garnished and the expediter takes it out. The malaxer needs to pay the most attention, give it the most love. I mean, every part of it takes love to make a really good oil, like everything else, right. But the malaxation period, well, that's where all the magic happens.

Over here's another of the really loud things in here, the centrifuge. So, when you break that emulsion in the malaxer, you extract oil from that pomace, it then goes through this centrifuge. Have you ever fucked up an aioli and seen this broken emulsion and it's all ugly and gross, with oils and fats and different shit floating around in there? Well, that centrifuge gets rid of all those solids and expels all those liquids (there's a ton of water in the olives, like in any fruit) and leaves you with just the oil.

I always break it down for people that we're making fruit juice here, right, which is why all these other parts come into play like the freshness, the way you process it, the way you store it – it's just like making fruit juice. A lot of people draw parallels to making wine but, really, wine doesn't exist in the grape. And there's all sorts of things can do to wine after you've made it – you can store it, you can age it, winemakers can add different things to it. Olive oil exists in the olive. We're just trying to not fuck it up and extract it as naturally and as quickly as possible.

Whole lotta juice

Now then, here's that iconic olive oil moment you've been waiting for, where you've got that neon yellow-green, high-visibility anti-freeze looking oil coming off the separator. Go on, you can just stick a cup underneath. See how cloudy it is, right? It looks like a soup broth or something because it's so cloudy, so thick, so funky. It's still alive – it's crazy.

At this point, if you taste it, you won't need to heat it up with your hands because the volatiles are already released, so you won't get too much nose off of it, but you'll get a lot on the palate. It's still really pungent oil and this one's a nice picual, a kind of ripe, typical mid- to late-harvest picual actually – you can tell because it isn't super fruity on the palate but it's still pretty pungent.

Because it's so turbulent there in the decanter and the separator, and the oil is still full of sediment and the air that has been pumped into it, it needs to settle, so it's pumped through to the tank room here. This, to me feels like the most peaceful room here – there's not so much noise and not much going on, save for the finished oil settling in giant stainless tanks that stretch all the way up to the ceiling with their nitrogen caps (oxygen's the enemy with this oil).

This is where I head to pick a bunch of different oils, grab samples and then take 'em back to the shack. I'm not sure if the oils settle completely here or if they get taken to settle at Lara where they bottle them, but it's a better tank farm that we take them to and that's where all the blending happens. For me, though, these single varietals are where it's at, and there are times where I strike gold – like the time I headed down there on a tip to tap tank 3003 for some really interesting, really beautiful Koroneiki. I have to be quick though, before they start slurping them out of the tanks and into the transport trucks – the end of the whole process you've just seen which, from start to finish, takes three to four days.

Right, we've seen enough, and it's getting stuffy in here. Let's get back outside under the stars and into that massive sea of trees.

Black Ball of Squid ink pasta dough

Overnight pumpkin

Serves 4–6

1 large kabocha squash (Japanese pumpkin)
   or Kent pumpkin
juice of 1 lemon
2–3 handfuls of fresh arugula (rocket)
2/3 cup (160 g/5½ oz) fresh ricotta
salt flakes

Almond dukkah

2 teaspoons cumin seeds
1 teaspoon fennel seeds
1 tablespoon white sesame seeds
½ teaspoon coriander seeds
2/3 cup (100 g/3½ oz) toasted almonds,
   finely chopped
salt flakes
extra-virgin olive oil, for drizzling

When I'm cooking at the shack I light a fire in the barbecue on the first morning I arrive, which I feed during the day and which is still warm the next morning when I go back to restart it (it's kind of this perpetual fire). I prep at the end of each evening around it for the next day, and when I call it a night it is always full of embers and big piles of warm ashes.

Now, I don't want to waste any of that energy, so one day during this cool-down period I experimented with what would happen if I just buried one of the many pumpkins that grow around the shack under the warm ashes, and this is the result. I cut the top of the pumpkin tableside, then I take out the seeds, mix in the oil, dukkah and everything else and it becomes this awesome warm pumpkin salad that's just super definitive of the place. It's one of my favorites.

Bury the pumpkin in the warm embers and ashes of a dying fire and leave it to cook overnight. (A completely covered pumpkin will take all night to cook and will most likely still be warm in the morning.)

The next day, test the doneness of the pumpkin with a cake tester all over (the tester should enter the pumpkin smoothly with little to no resistance). The pumpkin should be cooked through, but if any part of it needs more time, position that part towards the heat of the next day's fire. When completely cooked, carefully remove the pumpkin from the ashes, brushing off any extra ash.

For the dukkah, toast the cumin, fennel, sesame and coriander in a dry frying pan until aromatic, then transfer to a spice grinder or mortar and pestle and grind together to a rough powder. Mix the spice powder together with the chopped almonds, a sprinkling of salt and a drizzle or two of olive oil to help bind everything together.

Cut a circle out of the top of the pumpkin and remove the 'lid' by the stem. Scoop out the seeds and membrane and discard. Transfer the pumpkin tableside, add the dukkah, lemon juice, arugula, ricotta and a sprinkle of salt to the inside of the pumpkin and, with two large spoons, mix the ingredients together, carefully scraping pumpkin meat from the sides of the pumpkin into the mixture. Serve immediately.

Braised lamb shanks with gremolata

Serves 4

4 × 14–18 oz (400–500 g) lamb shanks
salt
extra-virgin olive oil
1 celery stalk, chopped
1 carrot, chopped
1 onion, chopped
1 garlic bulb, halved widthways
1 teaspoon black peppercorns
3 cups (750 ml/25½ fl oz) red wine
3 cups (750 ml/25½ fl oz) beef or chicken stock
2 bay leaves
2–3 thyme sprigs
2–3 rosemary sprigs

Gremolata

2 lemons
4 garlic cloves, finely sliced
⅓ cup (80 ml/2½ fl oz) extra-virgin olive oil
10–12 ripe, plump black raw Picual olives,
  ideally straight off the tree
1 cup (20 g/¾ oz) flat-leaf parsley leaves
freshly cracked black pepper

The gremolata here is a trick that Michele taught me for using the fresh picual olives that grow in the groves – smashing them and salting them before dumping a ton of fresh olive oil and fresh parsley over them really helps take away some of their bitterness, while sweating down the garlic here helps to really accentuate its sweetness, which makes for a great contrast. I don't really cook with fresh olives that much as they're not very palatable off the tree, but this is an execution that just works. It makes a perfect partner for a nice, fatty chunk of gamey lamb.

Preheat the oven to 325°F (160°C) or get a fire suitable for cooking going. Season the lamb shanks heavily with salt all over.

Warm a few glugs of olive oil in a Dutch oven (casserole dish) set over a high heat. Add the lamb shanks and sear until nicely browned on all sides. Setting the meat aside, add the celery, carrot, onion, garlic and peppercorns to the Dutch oven and cook over medium heat, stirring occasionally, until the veg begins to color.

Pour over the red wine and bring to a boil, scraping the bottom of the dish with a wooden spoon as you go to release all the sticky juices, then add the stock and return to the boil. Return the lamb shanks to the dish together with the herbs, pressing down on them with a spoon to make sure they are at least three-quarters submerged in the liquid. Spread over a layer of baking paper, cover with the lid and transfer to the preheated oven – or set next to the fire's embers placing a few coals on top – and cook for 2 hours, or until the meat is tender and falling off the bone and the braising liquid has significantly reduced. Remove from the heat and set aside to cool slightly.

While the lamb shanks cool, make the gremolata. Bring a small saucepan of water to a boil. Using a vegetable peeler, peel the zest from the lemons, then slice it as thinly as possible. Add the lemon zest slices to the pan of boiling water and blanch for 20 seconds, then strain. Repeat this process twice more so that the zest has been blanched three times in total (this will help remove any bitterness).

Slowly warm the garlic and olive oil together in a small saucepan. Smash the fresh olives to remove the pits and roughly chop the flesh before adding it to the pan with the garlic. Leaving the olive flesh to cook slightly, roughly chop the parsley leaves, then remove the pan from the heat and stir the parsley into the oil together with the blanched lemon zest, the juice of one of the zested lemons and plenty of freshly cracked black pepper.

To serve, divide the lamb shanks among plates, spooning over a little of the braising liquid followed by a liberal quantity of the warm gremolata.

Squid ink and spelt flour angel hair pasta with scallops roasted in their shells

Serves 6

5 cups (500 g/1 lb 2 oz) spelt flour
4 eggs
1 teaspoon fine salt
1 tablespoon squid ink
¼ cup (60 ml/2 fl oz) extra-virgin olive oil,
    plus extra for drizzling
3–6 tablespoons water
2 leeks, green tops discarded and white ends cut
    into thin rounds
12–18 scallops, cleaned and still in their shells
1 Buddha's hand citrus
3 tablespoons chopped chives
⅓ cup (20 g/¾ oz) chopped parsley
juice of 2 lemons

So the shack also serves as a place for the grove workers – whether Argentinian, Italian, American or Australian – to kind of unwind at times, a place to make some food and have those moments that you wouldn't have otherwise while you're away from home. And it turns out that, among them, Michele, Pablo and Herman are amazing cooks. So one night I decided I would make some squid ink pasta and put them all to work, making and shaping the pasta itself. While we all spoke different languages we were able to all work on rolling out the pasta dough and cutting it and cooking it together and it became our own language in the kitchen – along with glasses of wine, Jimi Hendrix and some classic rock, which we could all enjoy.

On a clean surface, measure out the spelt flour into an even mound. With your hands, create a bowl in the middle of the flour mound. Add the eggs, salt, squid ink, olive oil and 3 tablespoons of the water to the bowl and, using a fork, begin to mix the egg mixture together, slowly pulling in some of the flour. Continue to mix and pull in the flour until a dough starts to form, adding a little extra water if necessary, then knead the dough for a few minutes, or until the dough is pliable. Roll the dough into a ball, wrap tightly in plastic wrap and leave to rest in the refrigerator for 30 minutes.

Once rested, cut the dough into eight equal-sized portions. Roll one of the portions out with a rolling pin, then run it through your pasta machine and cut it according to its specifications. (If you don't have a pasta machine, roll the dough out as thinly as possible and cut it by hand.) Repeat with the remaining dough, being sure to dust the cut pasta with flour as you go to prevent sticking.

Warm a drizzle of olive oil in a small frying pan, add the leek rounds and a pinch of salt and cook until soft and caramelized, about 6–8 minutes. Set aside.

Place a grill grate about 12 in (30 cm) above hot, glowing coals, or heat your grill (barbecue) to medium.

Dress each scallop in its shell with a drizzle of olive oil, a light zesting of the Buddha's hand and a pinch of salt. Place the scallop shells on the grill and cook for about 3–4 minutes, until the liquid in the shells begins to bubble and the scallop flesh firms up.

Meanwhile, cook the pasta in a large pot of salted boiling water until al dente. Strain off the pasta, reserving a bit of the cooking water, then toss it together with the chives, parsley, caramelized leeks, lemon juice and a generous drizzle of oil, adding a little reserved pasta water if needed to loosen everything up.

To serve, pile the pasta into a large bowl and lay over the scallops in their shells to finish. Enjoy.

Late night lamb's fry

Serves 8

2–3 lamb's livers (approx. 7 oz/200 g each),
  fat and sinew removed
1 cup (250 ml/8½ fl oz) whole (full-cream) milk
½ cup (75 g/2¾ oz) all-purpose (plain) flour,
  seasoned with salt and pepper
extra-virgin olive oil, for drizzling
½ cup (70 g/2½ oz) pearl onions, halved
1 rosemary sprig, needles picked and roughly
  chopped
pinch of ground cayenne pepper
pinch of smoked paprika
1 shot (40 ml/1¼ fl oz) whiskey

This was a dish I made for the builder of the shack the night before the most wretched of hangovers. I never really cooked lamb's fry before but I'd cooked some similar things, so I treated it just like I would liver and onions, pouring a decent amount of whiskey over it while it was cooking on the plancha along with some cracked black pepper, onions and torn rosemary.

I spent the next little while walking around with the whisky bottle and that happy thought while they fed me beers and, well, that's when I learned I couldn't keep up with very blokey Australian dudes. We ended up all sleeping in the shack curled up by the fire that night and the next morning I was very thankful that I didn't have anybody coming for lunch that day.

Place the livers in a bowl, pour over the milk and leave to soak for 90 minutes.

Remove the soaked livers from the milk and pat dry, then slice into strips and toss through the seasoned flour. Pat any excess flour off the liver pieces and set aside on a plate.

Heat a griddle or a large cast-iron skillet over medium–high heat and add a drizzle of olive oil. Add the pearl onion halves and coated liver pieces to the griddle or pan and cook for 10 minutes until caramelized all over, turning and sprinkling over the rosemary, cayenne and paprika halfway through cooking. Pour over the whiskey, which will bubble and hiss (if you feel like showing off a bit at this point you can carefully light it with a match, if you want) and cook, stirring, until completely reduced and evaporated. Eat immediately with your fingers, accompanied by a few cold beers.

Olive oil ice cream with rhubarb and oats

Serves 6

Olive oil ice cream

1 1/3 cups (340 ml/11 1/2 fl oz) whole (full-cream) milk
1/4 cup (60 ml/2 fl oz) whipping (thickened) cream
1/4 teaspoon salt
1/2 cup (110 g/4 oz) sugar, plus 2 tablespoons
4 egg yolks
1/4 cup (60 ml/2 fl oz) extra-virgin olive oil, plus extra
  to serve

Rhubarb compote

3 cups (300 g/10 1/2 oz) rhubarb, cut into 1/2 inch
  (1 cm) chunks
1/2 cup (110 g/4 oz) sugar
1/4 teaspoon ground toasted cardamom
pinch of salt

Oat crumb

1/4 cup (25 g/1 oz) rolled oats
1/4 cup (25 g/1 oz) spelt flour
1/4 cup (55 g/2 oz) brown sugar
pinch of salt
2 tablespoons extra-virgin olive oil
2 egg whites, whisked

This was a bit of a no-brainer – olive oil works so well in an ice cream because an olive is just a fruit and it brings with it all those beautiful, fruity notes. The first time I made this ice cream I used a very green oil and I wanted to play off that greenness, so I served it up with chopped chervil and poached rhubarb and that evolved into this dessert riff – with the ice cream as the star of the show, the rhubarb acting as support and warm contrast, and a little bit of crumble over the top playing off that idea of a streusel or a pie.

To make the ice cream, add the milk, cream, salt and sugar to a heavy-based saucepan and bring to a gentle simmer, stirring, until the sugar is dissolved. In a separate mixing bowl, whisk together the egg yolks and an extra 2 tablespoons of sugar. Begin to temper the yolks by slowly whisking in the warm milk mixture, 1 tablespoon at a time. After you have whisked in 4–5 tablespoons, pour the egg mixture into the pan with the warm milk mixture and cook at a gentle simmer, stirring with a wooden spoon, until the mixture has thickened slightly and coats the back of a wooden spoon. Strain the thickened mixture through a fine-mesh sieve into a bowl set over an ice bath. Stir the mixture to cool quickly, then whisk in the olive oil. Churn this mixture for 1 hour in an ice cream maker, then pour into an airtight container and transfer to the freezer until needed (for best results, leave to freeze overnight).

For the rhubarb compote, toss the cut rhubarb in the sugar and leave it to sit in a saucepan for 30 minutes, then turn on the heat, bring to a simmer and cook for about 5 minutes, or until the pieces have softened but still largely retain their shape. Stir through the cardamom and salt and set aside.

Preheat the oven to 350°F (180°C) and line a baking sheet with baking paper.

To make the oat crumb, toss the oats, flour, sugar and salt together in a bowl with the olive oil. Mix in the egg whites until incorporated, then transfer to the fridge and leave for 10 minutes to firm. After refrigerating, spread the mixture evenly across the prepared baking sheet, transfer to the oven and bake for 20–30 minutes, stirring with a spatula occasionally, until golden and toasty. Remove from the oven and set aside until needed.

When ready to serve, place a spoonful of the warm rhubarb compote in the bottom of a serving bowl followed by a large scoop of the ice cream. Sprinkle over a little of the oat crumb and finish everything off with a last drizzle of olive oil. Repeat as many times as necessary.

5|26|11

I still can't believe I've been out here for almost two months.

I feel that if you had found me the first time I came out, before there was a shack – when it was still just a fire in the ground and that tiny shack with the propane burner inside of it – if you had told me I'd be spending two months of the year out here, I simply wouldn't believe it.

But look, here I am at the end of harvest. I made it. And it's been great.

I haven't been interacting with the guys down in processing as much this year. I don't really know what the difference is, except that before there were times when I'd look for excuses to visit friends like Mick and go and see what's up. Mick was constantly there – managing the crew, much like a sous chef would run the kitchen when the chef was out. I always liked checking in and being empathetic to whatever new hurdles he may be faced with that day.

I did go down today, though, and caught up with Pablo and some of the other guys.

You can tell towards the end of harvest that we're maybe not so bright-eyed and bushy-tailed as on the first day. Working down in processing is like having a new-born baby – if it cries, you have to be there, you have to be attentive – and so it's hard to stick to a normal schedule. There are some nights where you might not sleep as much, and I could tell that Pablo had been working pretty hard and was missing his family, his home.

It makes my feelings seem pretty miniscule, because these guys are here a lot longer than I am. Their sacrifices are a lot bigger than mine. They're missing out on their kids, their wives.

I just miss my friends and being a shithead in Sacramento.

It's pretty fascinating, too, to see the amount of people who come from around the globe to share one common interest, one common passion – it's extremely inspiring and reminds me of my times working in high-end restaurants like Saison and Coi, where the kitchen crews had traveled from around the world to work in those places because they were passionate and shared a common goal, a love. It's no different working a harvest with the crew at Cobram Estate.

Anyway, after seeing Pablo like that I made up a little treat package with a note and some lamb and caviar in it and took it down there for him. I know he will have enjoyed that.

More than anything, when I'm out here and have the time I love to go down to visit those guys to see it all working – those badasses who are all so passionate and professional about what it is we do here. When I go there it feels like a check-in, a reminder that there is something so much larger than what I do at the shack.

It's the bigger picture.

And it inspires and humbles me to know that, really, all I have to worry about is cooking and hosting and entertaining people. And that it's ok to fuck off all other responsibilities and just do that.

That's the root of everything I do out here and it's that that I'm drawn to and excited to return to.

That's the root of why I fell in love with food.

Sometimes what I miss most is
the therapy of chopping
wood every day

1. [France]

I've always felt the need to leave home to check out what I'm missing out on. To get out, to go see things. My first big trip away was after MiX, when it was becoming annoying, cooking for club people and, anyway, there was way more shit I wanted to do.

So that's when I decided I should probably go to France.

I don't know really what first inspired me or anything like that. It wasn't like I saw Julia Child and I was like, 'I have to go to France'. There wasn't any of that kind of stuff. I'd just kind of known that that's where I needed to go. I had a copy of Escoffier that was like a Bible to me. I read about Marco Pierre White and obsessed over him, which kind of first, and still does, fire up Michelin star dreams. Maybe that was part of the reason I wanted to go to France, because that's obviously where it all started.

The kitchens that I'd work in and the books that were suggested to me at the time by these chefs and then Marco Pierre White were probably my biggest influence to go to France. He would hop over to France when he was cooking and running restaurants, and check out what they were doing. Even before that, even before when he was a cook he would go to France for inspiration. And reading about that made it this pinnacle, this huge, I don't know, this great achievement to go there.

The Beatles · Flying

So, I told my family that's what I wanted to do. I gave this place that I was working at three months' notice – maybe I was lucky they didn't just fire me – and I moved into my grandma's house for a month before I went to France on a one-way ticket, which wasn't scary at all at the time.

Really, if I did that now I would be terrified. When you're older, you know how important family is and how important your roots are and how much you love where you live. But when you're a 19-year-old cook who wants to cook in the best restaurants in the world, you don't give a fuck about where you're from.

If I'm honest, the trip itself was a mixed bag. I spent time working at a Chateau in the countryside where I worked in the winery and vineyards, then traveled up north to the Dordogne region where I was promised restaurant work at a farm/B&B/brewery, but it ended up being slave labour for a fat Flemish dude who asked me to leave. But still, even if I didn't end up learning a whole lot more about food I met some incredible people, and I also had a great time hanging out with Tyler, who visited me in Monte Carlo. By that point I was completely broke and we spent the week sitting sharing 1 Euro cans of ravioli while watching the Bugatis, Ferraris and Lamborghinis drive by – we were so out of place and I loved it.

7/13/2009

I've neglected this wonderful, leather-bound gift my girlfriend gave me due to the (self-imposed) sense of burden that has been oozing out of it. The burden to write a novella, a step-by-step memoir of my time in France.

But I need an outlet; I need to let loose my thoughts, the happenings of the days, theories, musing, food stuffs and attempted sketches and, anyway, shouldn't that be the memoirs of my time here in France? What's happening here, right now, at Leni Dipple's place. Not some forced, piece of shit 'novella', anyway?

A friend gave me a word of advice today that I interpreted as 'let go of your past and all obligations at home'. Well, at least that's what I think she meant by 'find peace with the present and find your presence'. And she was right, I need to get off of the computer and stop thinking of 'when I get home'.

I need to remember why I'm here.

Quince condiment
with brie

I have a producer who delivers the most beautiful quince to the shack. They come by the bucketful and fill the entire kitchen with their aroma when she delivers them.

Generally, I like to process a lot of them – I'll peel and core them, cut them into chunks, put them into a pot with water and boil them down until they're nice and soft. At this point I'll add them to a food processor to make a purée, which I'll then put into a pot with equal parts sugar and cook gently for about two hours, or until it gets this beautiful dark pink color and has a thick, molten-like consistency. (If you want to do the same be sure to keep it at a very low temperature when you're cooking it down so the bottom doesn't burn and be aware that the bubbles that are popping can be a bit dangerous – it's almost like napalm.)

I use this quince condiment for a lot of different things. I put it in sauces to help thicken them, because quince has so much pectin in it. I'll also make quince barbecue sauces, or I'll add it to a mole to give it an extra layer of flavor. Or I'll just simply refrigerate it, cut cubes out of it and pop it onto a cheese plate.

One of the things I like to do most with this quince condiment, though, is to put it on some snacks that I make over the weekend. I'll take old bread or old baguette and put it onto the fire while I'm prepping, melt a bunch of cheese on top of it, then add this quince condiment along with some fresh torn herbs from the garden. This combo came about from me just looking at what food I had one day and wanting to make something edible, but it has turned out to be one of my favorite snacks.

1/31/19

Today I thought about that shitty beef course again. I mean, come on, it must have been, what, two years ago I served it up? And yet here I am, still thinking about it. Truth be told, I think about it once every other week or so.

It was one of those weird times where I wasn't confident in what I was doing, when I was between good times. I was uninspired and fell short and didn't execute to expectations, and to me it was apparent. I think the worst part was that my family was there and they knew it sucked and they still said it was good. I wanted to just kick everything.

That sort of event sticks with you for a long time. It's enough to make you want to run away.

2. [Montana]

I was 23 when we opened Blackbird in Sacramento, and I was the executive chef there for nearly two years, until I burned out and hid out in the mountains in Montana.

Blackbird was 100% art, 100% food, 100% GO, GO, GO. The owner was insane. She felt that, if we just hired artists and beautiful people to work in the restaurant, everything else would come together eventually. Like, surely there's something there? And there was. She was right, partially. But she also never hired a front of house manager because she didn't think that these beautiful and creative people should be managed.

It was a pretty wild time – as a chef, having the carte blanche to do whatever I wanted to do with the food was great and I really got to feel things out for myself, but I burned out HARD, partly because of that lack of a manager but also because I was the only one in that place who had fine dining knowledge. I was like, 'you guys can't be doing this shit' quite often. The level of food we were serving did not match the service and that's what everyone around town was saying. Best food in town, worst service in town. But everyone was really cool. And if your server's hella cool and the bartender is a painter you know and you went to his gallery opening, well, if he's a shit bartender you're not going to care as much because you're enjoying the food and the overall experience.

And of course, we all got together and partied every night and got weird all the time, so I was burning the candle at both ends. The others would all come in for a five or six hour shift but I was pulling a sixteen every day, and it got to the point where I was so burned out that I became really volatile and reactive – somebody would fuck up something small and it would feel like everything was just ruined. I remember making someone cry one day and thinking 'ok, this is not cool, I've got to get the fuck out of here'. And then I just couldn't physically do it anymore.

A good morning is a camp
oven buried in Hot coals

Chasing Harvest

I remember making that decision to leave. I had driven Holly, my girlfriend at the time, to the airport in San Francisco as she was going to Belize. I drove her in her car, a new Volvo Sedan, which, at the time for me this was like, a really nice car, because I either didn't have a car or I was driving a '91 Subaru.

So, I got all that stuff done, said goodbye to her and had the rest of the day off. I had to take her to the airport at four in the morning or something stupid like that, and it was still dark, so I decided to take a long way home and I drove up to Bodega Bay, up to the coast.

Holly had just gone to Belize, I had friends who were doing so much awesome stuff, seeing the world and travelling, or else just doing nothing, hanging out, smoking pot and drawing in some dead-end job. <u>I was so jealous of that second group because they could just clock out and they were done – they didn't have to worry about anything. (Truth be told, I'm still a little envious of people like that, sometimes.)</u>

Anyway, I drove up the coast and landed on Salmon Creek beach for sunrise. It was the most beautiful I have ever seen the beach – the tide was all the way out, the sun was coming up and the sunrise was reflecting these orange, pink, purple hues all across this wet, seal-like skin of a beach where the ocean had been just hours before. There were still little holes spilling out water, little swirls, seaweeds and rocks and things still bubbling, fizzing, just kind of waking up with the rest of the world. It was misty and hazy but perfectly clear because it was sunrise. It was just stunning.

And I thought, you know what? I'm going to sit here for a little bit and hang out. I had an AMPM coffee in a big Styrofoam cup and found this beach chair – one of those ones with the cupholders – toppled over and covered in sand. I picked it up and shook it off, then stuck the cup in the cupholder, sat down to roll a joint and really felt like, 'what are you doing?'. 'You're 23 years old, you've been working in kitchens for almost 10 years. You moved to France for a little bit and that was cool, but what else are you doing'? I was so jealous of the rest of the world's freedom. I didn't realize it just then, that being tied into a kitchen wasn't for me. But I did start to feel that something wasn't right.

Still, I had my plan for the day sorted. I was going to go home and I was going to go into work later that afternoon, even though it was my day off – that's what I did, I was Chef. But instead I found myself going on and on all the way to Fort Bragg. I stopped. I went through the redwoods. I touched the trees. I splashed through puddles, just enjoying myself with this childlike sense of wonder and freedom. And I just kind of realized, like, I had such a good time just driving and exploring. Since then I've been back to these places a ton of times, but back then, I had only been there in my childhood. I'd never had the chance to go there a ton of times, even though it was an hour and a half away, because I'd been working my ass off. So I naturally wondered, what is all this worth?

I didn't form these thoughts fully until all those years later after I left Saison. But that's kind of the inception point for those thoughts. I went through the trees, I went through the forest and I remember thinking, if there's one small piece of earth that's so close to home that's so beautiful and so rewarding, well... how much else am I missing out on?

So I quit and went to Montana with Holly. Rode horses. Shot guns. Foraged. Cooked. Fell back in love with cooking. And that was the really wild thing. I fell in love with food at a very early age. I fell in love with fine dining. I fell in love with all of that. But I had broken away from it.

I didn't cook anything for a while, though. First I started foraging, started hunting, started fishing. But getting hold of all these amazing ingredients meant I was able to slowly fall in love with food all over again. One night, after I had started cooking again a little, Holly's mom had some friends over for dinner and they said 'wow, you're a really good chef!'. They hadn't expected it because I was just, you know, Holly's boyfriend and she's just some rich punk who went to some liberal art school and thought it would be fun to be a cook. But they were like, wow you can actually cook. I was like, 'yeah I had this restaurant for a little bit' and they were like, 'really?'. 'What the fuck!'. 'Like, what are you doing here?!'.

They were just blown away. Remember, I was a 23-year-old punk ass, but they started introducing me to people and I slowly created this network of foodie people – most of them had worked for the Yellowstone foundation – and that's when we started to get together and started hunting and gathering and getting a ton of product back to our place. Foraging a lot, getting into books, getting new books to look into. Going on hikes from sunrise to sunset. Foraging any time of day. Creating stockpiles. Going home at night and preserving it (and raiding Holly's mom's crazy well-stocked wine cellar while we were at it), then inviting people over to share everything at these dinners I started to organize. Before I knew it I had found myself roaming the countryside and cooking again with the whole thing culminating in this little scene we'd created.

Now that I think back, it was the same as in France, where towards the end of my stay I had been organising dinners every Sunday for this group of friends I'd met to show them what modern American cooking could be. That had started pretty tongue-in-cheek, 'I'm going to show you fuckers that American food isn't just cheeseburgers!' and they were also like, 'Wow, you're a pretty good cook. Let's do this again next week. I'll bring nectarines. I'll bring Cognac. I'll bring whatever'. The dinners just started coming together. That same shit happened in Montana. I love it how food can do that – how it can just reach out and make connections with people and that sort of thing can just develop organically.

When the weather turned cold it came time to go back home to Sacramento, but I still remember Montana as being the place that helped reintroduce me to the idea of cooking as unconditional love. Since then, that same sort of thing has happened several times, this leaving home and returning with new inspiration – this continued falling out and falling in love with food and cooking – but that was the first time I had fallen in love with food again. It felt so good.

Good ol'-fashioned lover boy

kneading is meditative

Bone marrow

I first cooked up bone marrow in my first year at the shack. I was at the butcher in Robinvale – who's my lifesaver at least once a week – and I saw some large femur bones in the back, so I asked if I could have a few to experiment just putting them in the fire to see what happens. (When I'm out at the shack I just see shit and, you know, introduce it to the fire in a certain way to see if it works.)

Anyway, I put the bones in the fire and kept rotating them and at the end of the lunch I set up a little table by all the guests and I took these huge charred, gnarly bones and started sawing them in half with a small hack saw. I asked the table if they all liked bone marrow and everyone said hey, so I mixed it up with just a bit of lemon zest, some herbs from the garden and some super fresh, very robust oil to stand up to the marrow's fatty intensity, then put it on grilled toast and actually hand-fed the toast bites to everybody as a little finishing touch. I've been cooking bone marrow over the fire a few different ways since, but this is still my favorite.

Quinoa and prawn tamale with tomatillo salsa verde

Serves 12

4 cups (740 g/1 lb 10 oz) cooked quinoa
4 large eggs
3 tablespoons extra-virgin olive oil, plus extra
  for drizzling
pinch of salt
approx. 2 cups (300 g/10½ oz) raw prawn (shrimp)
  meat, no shells
2–3 splashes of heavy (thick/double) cream,
  if needed
12 green banana leaves

Salsa verde

1½ lbs (675 g) tomatillos, husks removed
1 white onion, chopped into large pieces
3 garlic cloves
2 jalapeño peppers, seeds and ribs removed
pinch of salt
2 tablespoons extra-virgin olive oil, plus extra
  for drizzling
½ cup (15 g/½ oz) cilantro (coriander) leaves,
  plus extra for serving
juice of 1 lime

To serve

radish slices
fresh lime wedges

This was inspired by my missing Californian-Mexican food while in Oz, and the idea behind it came about when I found tomatillos at a local farmers' market, which made me think of tamales. Now, obviously I didn't have masa or corn husks there, but I was able to get hold of quinoa together with banana leaves from the Asian food market. I cooked the quinoa and mixed it with some egg to try and emulate the structure of a prepared masa, then I piled it into the leaves and piped a prawn mousse inside of it and folded them up, then chucked them into the fire.

When I pulled these aromatic, smouldering banana leaf parcels out of the fire I was stoked to see the quinoa had crisped up and the filling inside was perfectly cooked. To finish, I layered them up with the tomatillo salsa verde and some sliced radish and cilantro – fundamentals of Mexican cuisine that are really easy to find in California, but not something a lot of the people at the shack had before.

For the salsa verde, toss the tomatillos, onion, garlic, jalapeños and salt together in a bowl with a drizzle of olive oil. Tip the mix into a roasting rack to roast directly over hot coals until everything is well caramelized and the tomatillos are beginning to deflate, then transfer to a blender or food processor together with the cilantro and lime juice and blitz on high, slowly adding the olive oil as you go, until all the oil is incorporated and the salsa is smooth. Set aside to cool.

Mix the cooked quinoa, eggs, olive oil and salt together in a bowl. Set aside in the fridge until needed.

Add the prawn meat to a food processor and pulse until smooth and spreadable, adding a drizzle of olive oil and a few splashes of cream if the mixture is looking too firm. Season the mixture with salt, then transfer to a piping bag.

To build the tamales, tear the banana leaves into roughly 8 × 6 in (20 × 15 cm) rectangles, keeping the torn excess. Place a few spoonfuls of the chilled quinoa mixture into the middle of one of the banana leaf rectangles in the shape of a smaller rectangle, then pipe a line of the prawn mixture down the center. Roll the banana leaf up into a tight cylinder, tying off each end with the reserved torn leaf strips, then repeat with the rest of the leaves and filling.

Once all the tamales are formed and tied, prepare a medium-heat coal bed from the fire. You'll want a surface of coals, mixed with ash, that can accommodate all of them.

Lay the tamales onto the hot coals and cook for 4 minutes, turning halfway, or until the banana leaf begins to burn away from the filling a bit.

To serve, divide the tamales among plates, cut away some of the banana leaf, spoon over the salsa and garnish with sliced radish and a few extra cilantro leaves. Accompany with lime wedges for squeezing.

4/21/17

I like to go around and eat everything. I want to eat ten great meals a day if I can.

And I was able to in Thailand.

I'd ride my scooter down to the next beach and get a rum and soda and a couple of bites. And the days were just spent tasting and drinking and putting my feet up and relaxing.

Burning Spear - Any River

My neighborhood beach bar, owned by a cool old man in a skirt

3. (Thailand)

It was last year, after harvest and Australia, that I headed to Thailand. It was, I think, my first real vacation (it was different from when I left Blackbird and went to Montana because back then I was leaving the job and it was the end of something). This gave me a taste of that relaxation which I guess is what a vacation does for everybody. Real time away from life. And it was amazing.

Well, it didn't really catch up to me until I was in Koh Samui which was my second stop. I started off in Bangkok. Everything was so intense, it was like this sensory overload and I was like a dog let off a leash because I'd been in the groves alone for so long – in the middle of nowhere for so long – to be picked up and dropped into this hive of scooters and neon and food and music and all sorts of crazy shit that I hadn't experienced for so long was heavy.

It was exciting too, and I got to party for the first time in a long time.

I headed to Khao San Road – the place that every backpacker goes to party in Bangkok. It's the Gomorrah of Thailand. Everyone's drinking in the streets, every club has people spilling out into the street, they all have loud music and they all have hot girls to try and get you to come inside, come party, come spend money. The road was basically blocked off and it was just a sea of people in the street, going nuts. They were selling beer in the street and people were doing whip-it balloons that they fill with nitrous and shit like that.

I ended up hanging out with these six girls. There was such a language barrier it was so stupid, it wasn't worth it, but we were sitting down and ordering buckets of drinks – there's this bar that you can order a bucket at, like the ones you would take to the beach to build a sandcastle in, a plastic pail with a handle and everything. You pick your spirit and mixer like a basic well drink, but they put it in that bucket with a big old straw in there.

So, we ordered all these buckets and everyone there on the street is trying to sell you shit, everybody, like shoving things in your face and you have to be really stern and say no. But it was hard to say no to all this stuff after being in the groves. It was my first time in Southeast Asia, my first actual vacation, and my first night in Bangkok. So I had a lot of buckets. Many, many buckets.

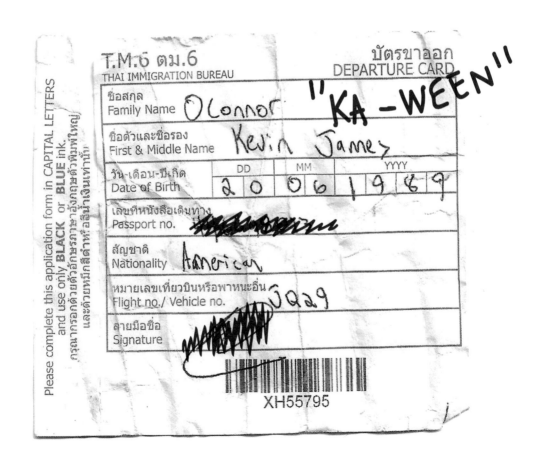

tuk tuk

Chasing Harvest

At this point, three of the girls from the group peeled off and I was hanging out with three of them still but had, kind of, set my sights on one of them. So I went to this club and ordered a gin and tonic and they gave me a bottle of gin and they asked how many glasses I wanted. I'm like, 'ok, I'd like three glasses'. And it was just, like, insanely cheap, too. Super dangerous. Meanwhile, there's people trying to sell me scorpions on a stick, bracelets that have profanities woven into them and just the most random shit.

After eating a scorpion (crunchy, but not delicious) and drinking some more I took the girl I had my eye on back to my place, though god knows how, as I blacked out by the time we got there.

Anyway, I wake up the next morning and she's in my bed. We are both fully clothed. She didn't speak any English, at all. So I, um, we were using Google Translate a little bit the night before to flirt, which, you know, takes a lot of the lust out of flirting. I mean, who knows? Half the time I don't know if she actually got what I'm trying to say, but it doesn't matter, we were dancing. So now I had to ask Google Translate to ask if we had sex. She just laughed hysterically. You did not need to translate the fact that I fucking fell asleep.

You know when you wake up and you're either still drunk or you're so out of your element you don't allow yourself to be hungover and then all of a sudden you do and it's like a freight train, and you're like, 'what the ████ just happened to me? It's like someone just hit me in the back of a head with a shovel'. It was that, but add to that being in Bangkok was like being in a ████ diaper. It's humid and fucking hot. And the city… it smells. There aren't emission standards in Thailand. There's just like a million scooters vomiting black smoke and leaving little dust clouds when you're having the worst hangover of your entire existence.

So, I call the girl a cab and I'm like, I need to get out of here. I need to get coffee, I need to get food, I need to get water – I need to get all these pieces that I put together for my hangover cure that I've got better at developing over the years. So I go down this elevator for ever and go out onto the streets. Look, Bangkok is the worst place in the world to be hungover. The worst place that I've been to be hungover. You've got your hangover, it smells like shit, it's hot, it's humid, and all these scooters are loud as.

There were all these shrines around town; they're on every other corner – like a Buddha or a very ornate miniature church-looking shrine – and it's as common to see one as it is to see a newspaper box. So I'm walking into the fucking 7-11 and I'm seriously, like, I kept stopping and holding my head and just supporting myself up and I'm like, 'oh my god. What if I just laid down on the ground? What if I just sat in that shade for a little while? Maybe? What if I just closed my eyes?' So, so, so bad. I was so hungover I came to my knees at one of those shrines and I said 'give me the strength to get to this goddamn 7-11'.

So I got to my knees and just whispered into the shrine for a bit…

It took a while, but I finally got my shit together. I explored Bangkok a little more. I got a haircut and ate a bunch of street food. I was just obsessed with the street food. That was what I was most excited about. That's what I remember from watching Anthony Bourdain when I was a kid and I was just like 'he's on a scooter, he's eating street food, this is fucking cool!'. Thailand looked great. And the moment I starting doing that I was like, wow, I'm here. I'm doing exactly what I dreamed of without really realising that I had been dreaming about it.

You know how most dreams are measurable, attainable dreams, but this one was one I didn't understand existed until I was actually living it.

One of the few places I didn't sweat
- the river taxis

If Bangkok didn't really make sense because I was there so fast and it was so intense, so different from where I had been, then Koh Samui was the first time I got to really kick back and feel I was away on vacation. It's an island and it was so gorgeous there that all I wanted to do was relax. I didn't want to go party, I didn't want some commercialized anything, I just wanted to stay put and put my feet up. And the moment I did, that's when I was really like, 'woah I'm actually on vacation'. It's a weird feeling if you're not used to it, and it only really hit me on day or two or three when I realized that I really didn't have to do anything if I didn't want to. I didn't have to go to an airport, I didn't have to cook if I didn't want to (though I wanted to, because the markets were insane) I didn't have to go on this or that hike if I didn't want to. There were no obligations. A big part of that was the fact that I was alone – I didn't have anyone holding me accountable to doing anything.

Don't get me wrong, there was lots of opportunity to be with people and do stuff. But as soon as I got there I was like, 'you know what? Nothing is more important than just being here by myself, enjoying this and being present and not following this conquest of booty and booze and all that'.

My place in Koh Samui was really weird. I hung out, well, stayed in two houses by accident. Arriving, it took me for ~~fucking~~ ever to get out of the airport because there's no address to the place that I'm staying, I couldn't get hold of the owner and I thought the whole thing was a scam (I even sent him a message saying 'look if this is a scam just tell me so I can find a new place') but I guess he just had bad service as he eventually got back to me and ended up being a really awesome dude – a big muscular, bald Buddhist Russian guy who had lived on the island for ten years or so.

Still, I didn't know how to find the place, so this taxi driver who I finally arranged at the airport took me to meet him at a 7-11. I get into the back of this weird big taxi van – it's got all these crazy lights and all this wild shit and curtains on the windows – and it's nearly sunset, so the lighting is gorgeous and I'm just driving along the coast in the back of this big taxi van to meet up with, and then follow, this big Russian guy on a scooter down this supremely sketchy road. It's at this point that I kind of start to realize that, hmm, this is just a bit dodge and I'm a little bit scared. It's very quiet, the rain had stopped and it was eerie and everything was wet and there was a lot of buzzing with the bugs and stuff, but other than that it was silent, you know.

Sketch island turned paradise

So I get to this house and the dude introduces himself and, well, he has some crazy, googly eyes. I feel bad saying that because he ended up being such a really nice guy, but you can imagine the scene – a giant bald, buff, tank-topped Russian with googly eyes in the middle of nowhere on this island in Thailand. It's at times like this that you start to think about the shit your dad told you about being safe while you're out there.

Anyway, surprised to find it's just me in the back of that van, he meets me at the gate to the courtyard, pushes it open, throws his arms out and says 'You have entire villa to yourself!'. It was super cool – two houses, a pool in between them and enough rooms for a ton of people. He shows me around, offers to rent me his scooter, which I accept, tells me where the beach is at and gives me the rundown of the island (which is small, has one main street and can be gotten around in about two hours on the scooter), including his favorite restaurants and a rum distillery in the center of the island.

It was so weird having that entire villa to myself.

I was so happy and so content to be alone, but almost making fun of myself for being in some place that was so luxurious by myself. It felt weird not enjoying it with somebody else, to the point that I started to pretend that people were there enjoying it with me. The pool was situated between the two houses, so each morning I'd wake up and swim through the pool to the other side, pretending that I was going to greet my friends who were staying in the other house. 'Oh, let me swim over to Ben and Jess's house'. I didn't want desperately to enjoy it with someone else but it just didn't make sense to enjoy it by myself because I had never done that before.

Mikey Dread - Positive Reality

I made a lot of food in Koh Samui. I ate a lot the first couple of days and then I started diving into indoor-outdoor markets, which were set up like something that we would call a farmers' market, with a lot of product stuffed into one place.

I found so much shit I'd never cooked with before. I learned to ask if you need to cook it or if you need to eat it raw, because that's kind of the basic – like, if you take something home and you don't know what you're getting into, you don't eat it raw and if you should eat it raw, then you don't want to cook it. Once my knowledge and experience of Thai food developed, specifically of the sauces and poultices and condiments that they grind up in the mortar and pestle, I added a third question, 'or do you make it into a paste'? Do you pound it into a sauce?

Because it was like, you'd eat something and it would be delicious. But you couldn't chew it. If you cooked it, it would be like cooking parsley or something – it would just not be great cooked. A lot of times it was herbs that you just throw into a mortar and pestle and pound. So it was interesting to adapt my conversation to the style of food that they had there, and as an outsider – and not knowing too much about Thai food – it changed my ideas up.

Using Thai ingredients and this new understanding of Thai food but not making Thai food was a lot of fun. I'd go to markets and taste things and compare them to things and kind of take note of what role they'd play in a dish, how they feel on the palate and then apply that to the way I cook.

For example, I found some grilled baby corns and I made this very French sauce but it had dried shrimp, shallot, bacon and chili in it. Kind of savory. I noticed too how there were lots of parallels that I could draw to Latin food with the heat and the tartness and the citrus and the proximity to the ocean, you know, you can draw to other cultures and different foods… so it wasn't like, wow, now I'm really inspired to cook Thai food, it was just a huge inspiration to just cook and dive through the markets and discover different ingredients and kind of put yourself back into an experimental stage.

It felt so good.

Meat on a stick and plastic baggies forever

Freshly pounded curry pastes

Spiced syrup cocktail

Makes 1 cup (250 ml/8½ fl oz)

1 cup (220 g/8 oz) pure cane sugar
1½ cups (375 ml/12½ fl oz) water
6 whole cloves
1 whole star anise
1 teaspoon black peppercorns
1 whole cinnamon stick
6 allspice berries
approx. 2 in (5 cm) fresh orange peel

While on Koh Samui I spent a lot of my time scootering around, including to the rum distillery that my Russian dude had told me about. Run by an old French guy, it was one of the most beautiful properties on the island – an old mansion with a beautifully manicured lawn (you don't see a lot of lawns in Thailand) and gorgeous landscaping. As I pulled in on my tiny scooter it felt like some drug cartel's lair.

Anyway, the guy there was not only making rum from sugar cane but he was also making this spiced syrup from the cane too. Smooth and delicious, he'd serve you a shot of it that you'd sip with a small glass of the syrup on the side, almost like a little chaser. The guy showed me round the distillery, which itself was pretty cool – all vintage equipment, stuff from the super old rum producer who he had originally purchased the place from. After trying a lot of rum there that day, I bought some more of it along with the syrup and took it back to my villa, where I filled a coconut with it, squeezed a lime into it, sat by the pool and talked to my imaginary friends.

This syrup is an approximation of that one, as the guy told me the recipe verbally so I can't be sure I got it all down. But it's close enough, I reckon.

Stir together all the ingredients in a saucepan. Continuing to stir constantly, bring to a boil, then reduce the heat to a simmer and let it ride for 40 minutes, or until the syrup has reduced to about 1 cup (250 ml/8½ fl oz). Pour into a container and leave to cool for immediate use. (The syrup will keep in an airtight container in the fridge for up to 1 week.)

Spiced syrup bananas

Serves 4

4 gluay naam waa bananas, or other short fat
   bananas, just ripe
¼ cup (60 ml/2 fl oz) Spiced Syrup (see page 206)
coconut or vanilla ice cream, to serve (optional)

Thailand is where I saw people cooking bananas in their peels over fire for the first time. Obviously, being a fire fiend I was like, 'fuck, I can do that – it's literally a banana sitting in its peel over the fire that is being turned every once in a while'. The bananas sort of slow roast in their own juice over the coals, which barely cooks them but sort of changes their texture and creates this yummy syrup that's kind of sweet and beautiful. Brushing the lot with my spiced syrup gives them this Bananas Foster vibe and makes them pretty irresistible.

Place a grill grate about 10–12 in (25–30 cm) above hot, glowing coals, or heat your grill (barbecue) to medium–high.
   Place the bananas directly onto the grill grate and cook, turning occasionally for 25 minutes, until the skins have begun to darken substantially, the banana is soft and the sugar inside it has started to boil out of small holes in the skin. Remove the bananas from the coals, peel and liberally baste with the spiced syrup. Eat immediately with coconut or vanilla ice cream, if you like.

By Chiang Mai I'd come to terms with being sweaty all the time, so I dressed for the occasion in pretty much the way you'd imagine any white dude would in Thailand – short sleeves, collared shirt unbuttoned 99 per cent of the way. A couple of necklaces, some beads, hair just slicked back constantly from the sweat and ocean water. I had a kind of red face from drinking too much rum in the sun and some cuts and bruises and scrapes here and there from little scooter crashes, and hardened feet from always wearing sandals or going barefoot.

It was a really good vibe.

I was looking forward to being off the island and exploring another large city. I'd heard that the food was better up north and it lived up to its reputation. Chiang Mai was cool. The markets there were a lot bigger. Huge. I mean, they had a night market every night where they'd shut down the street and there'd be vendors selling anything from knock-off Calvin Klein underwear to really good grilled lobster and salt baked fish and produce and noodles and pad thai – obviously, stuff like that made to order and people making dumplings to order and all sorts of different drinks that were sold in bags. Everything is put in a bag. They like to give you plastic bags because you can loop them under your scooter. You know, every scooter has little hooks, so it's not uncommon to see a family of three or four, with an infant hanging on to the front with four bags of groceries on the scooter.

But then I got the call that my Aunt Lori had died. I knew that she'd been sick but I… underestimated it. My mom can be very emotional. So I didn't really realize the severity of my aunt being in hospital. You're not there, so it's kind of like, '██ I hope they're ok' and then you kind of continue going about being on vacation in Thailand by yourself – shooting from the hip, having to figure out where the ██ you are, having to communicate with people, having to figure out each meal, having to set an itinerary as you go… and all the other things that go into traveling.

My brother told me. My mom couldn't tell me, of course. I mean, her best friend died unexpectedly.

It was so weird. I was already in a space where I didn't feel that anything was real and I didn't have anybody to pinch me. I didn't have anybody to reference crazy shit that I saw or beautiful things that I experienced. I didn't have that checking system, like 'did you just see that?' 'Yeah, that was beautiful'. You experience all that by yourself to a point where it's almost like a dream sequence, because you're just by yourself, and immediately it turned into a nightmare. It was just unbelievable.

I'm away in a physically stunning, young, vibrant, fun, exotic city that's full of amazing food. It's my heaven. And my family back home is in hell in a fucking hospital.

Grilled baby corn

Serves 6

14–18 baby corn
2 tablespoons extra-virgin olive oil, plus extra
   for drizzling
salt
2 shallots, sliced into thin rings
2 tablespoons dried shrimp
2 tablespoons water
juice of 2 limes
2 teaspoons dried chili powder
6 ngo gai (also known as recao or long cilantro/
   coriander) leaves or a handful of regular cilantro
   (coriander) leaves, torn

This is my unintentional riff on elotes, a Mexican corn dish that I kind of figured out was the direction I was going in as I was halfway through cooking it for the first time. Elotes are slathered in mayonnaise, chili, lime and parmesan – so there's saltiness, creaminess, a bit of acidity and a bit of heat – and you get the same kind of thing here. The dried shrimp has this salty, almost smoky bacon-like kick to it (and we all know that bacon and corn is great together) and then adding the shallots, which you see a lot in Thailand, especially dried shallot, lime juice and chili help to bring out the elotes vibe.

I really encourage anybody who hasn't before to try cooking with dried shrimp and dried shallots as they are a really awesome way to add flavor to a lot of different dishes, and not just Thai food. This one may be a weird mix of Thai, Californian and Mexican flavors, but it definitely works.

Fire up your grill (barbecue) and get it nice and hot.
   Toss the baby corn in a drizzle of olive oil along with a few pinches of salt. Transfer to the grill and cook for 10–15 minutes, or until charred all over.
   While the corn is cooking, sweat the shallots down in the olive oil in a wok or large frying pan until softened and translucent.
   Stir the dried shrimp and water into the pan, then add the grilled corn and mix everything together well. Add the lime juice, chili powder, and torn herb leaves and toss to combine, then serve immediately.

Clams in Chang

Serves 6–8

1 shallot, sliced into thin rings
2 tablespoons extra-virgin olive oil
1½ cups (225 g/8 oz) cherry tomatoes, halved
2 garlic cloves, smashed
3–4 lb (1.35–1.8 kg) clams
1 × 11 fl oz (330 ml) bottle Chang or other light beer
1 heaped tablespoon palm sugar
2 teaspoons fish sauce
¼ cup (10 g/¼ oz) dill fronds
¼ cup (10 g/¼ oz) Thai basil leaves
2 limes

Steamers – mussels and clams cooked in beer – are something that I've been enjoying and cooking my entire life. Growing up I used to go camping, pull some mussels from the beach and chuck them in the pot. It's something that's so simple and so satisfying to make and eat.

This Thai version, which I made while staying there, kind of has the same vibe as what would happen at home if I were to cook clams and mussels on the beach with a couple of beers. I just grabbed a beer from the twelve pack that I had in the fridge and added it to the pan with the few things I had sitting around in the fridge or the pantry. The clams I had when I made it there were gorgeous ones that I'd never worked with before – I couldn't tell you the name of the variety but they were a cool, funky looking blue and were super sweet and delicious – but really this will work with any clam you can get your hands on.

In a wok or large pot start sweating the shallots in the olive oil until soft and translucent. Add the tomatoes, garlic cloves and clams and cook, stirring regularly, for 30 seconds, then add the beer and the palm sugar and steam until the clams have popped open, about 4–6 minutes. Remove from the heat, stir in the fish sauce, fresh herbs and lime juice (throwing the juiced limes into the mix to scent the broth if you like) and serve in the pot with a few more beers on the side.

Coconut-cooked pumpkin, kaffir lime and fruity olive oil

Serves 4

1 medium kabocha squash (Japanese pumpkin)
   or Kent pumpkin, peeled and cut into
   1 in (2.5 cm) chunks
20 fl oz (585 ml) coconut milk
2 kaffir lime leaves
zest of ¼ kaffir lime
fruity extra-virgin olive oil, to serve

It took me a while to figure out how to buy coconut milk in Thailand; it's not something you see out on display, but is instead kind of stashed away in these ice chests and is sold – like everything else in Thailand – in little plastic bags tied with rubber bands. Freshly made that day, basically to order, it was a really exciting ingredient to me, so once I discovered how to ask for it and get it I really started playing around with it, to see what I could do with it.

Up in the city of Chiang Mai in the north of Thailand a lot of the vegetable stands at that time were selling what looked like kabocha squash or small Japanese pumpkins, so I experimented with peeling and cooking the pumpkin in the coconut milk for a really long time with a little kaffir lime for some aromatics and some really fruity, fresh Australian olive oil I'd smuggled into Thailand with me. It was the first time I ever cooked pumpkin in coconut and they played well.

Add the squash, coconut milk and kaffir lime leaves to a heavy-based or cast-iron pot and bring to the boil, then transfer the pot to the stovetop over a low heat (or above a fire, if you like). Simmer for 40–60 minutes, or until the squash has become very tender and the coconut milk has reduced substantially and taken on an amber hue.
   Transfer the thickened coconut milk and pumpkin mixture to a serving dish, sprinkle over the lime zest and finish with a drizzle of fruity olive oil to aromatize. Serve either as a sweet side dish or as a dessert.

Salt-crusted snapper and green papaya salad

Serves 4

1 × 3 lb (1.35 kg) whole snapper, gutted
2 lemongrass stems, halved lengthwise
3 garlic cloves
2–3 Thai bird's eye chiles
1 in (2.5 cm) piece of ginger, roughly chopped
1 cup (290 g/10 oz) kosher salt
1 tablespoon all-purpose (plain) flour
1 tablespoon water

Papaya salad

juice of 2½ limes
2 tablespoons extra-virgin olive oil
2 tablespoons fish sauce
3 garlic cloves, very finely chopped
3 tablespoons palm sugar
1 red Thai bird's eye chili, sliced into thin rings
1 green papaya, peeled and cut into matchsticks
1 green mango, peeled and cut into matchsticks
½ cup (15 g/½ oz) each of cilantro (coriander),
 mint and Thai basil leaves
½ cup (80 g/2¾ oz) toasted chopped peanuts
6 snake (yardlong) beans, cut in 2 in (5 cm) pieces

I saw a lot of fish being cooked on the streets of Thailand, especially when I was on the island of Koh Samui. I was really interested in seeing how the stallholders were cooking it, and this method I saw for cooking whole fish – stuffing them with lemongrass and ginger, covering them in a salt crust and then putting them on a spit and rotating them over a half barrel of charcoal – was one of my favorites. The smell was intoxicating and watching those salt-crusted fish spin around with spears of lemongrass protruding from their mouths was both hypnotic and drool-worthy. I was a little intimidated to buy one at the time because I didn't know what to do with it once I got it into my hands there at the side of the road, so instead I took a stab at something similar when I was back at the house I was staying at (though rather than use the rotisserie I just flipped the fish occasionally over this charcoal barbecue I had there).

One of my favorite Thai dishes is the green papaya salad som tum, and I love the fact that every different stand there would make it a little bit different. I made my own version of it by marrying it together with this salt-crusted snapper, flaking the flesh off of the carcass and folding it into all these crunchy, spicy, sweet and herbaceous ingredients to end up with this beautiful toothsome salad.

Fire up a charcoal grill (barbecue) and let it burn down to medium–low heat coals.

Stuff the cavity of the fish with the lemongrass, garlic, chiles and ginger. Stir together the salt, flour and water in a bowl to make a paste-like mixture then, using your hands, smear the mix all over the fish, plastering the entire body from head to tail. Lay the coated fish on the grill and cook for 40–50 minutes, or until the flesh is firm and the salt crust is golden-brown all over. Try to flip the fish as little as possible during this time – you want to allow enough time for the salt to dry out and create a hard crust.

While the fish is cooking, prepare the salad. Make the dressing by whisking together the lime juice, olive oil, fish sauce, garlic, palm sugar and sliced chili. In a mixing bowl, toss together the papaya, mango, herbs, peanuts and beans. Add the dressing to the bowl, toss again and leave to marinate as the fish finishes cooking.

When ready, remove the cooked fish from the grill and leave it to rest for 5–10 minutes, then take off the salt crust with your hands and carefully begin to peel back the skin from the flesh. With a fork and working one side at a time, flake the fish flesh off the bones, then mix it into the salad. Serve immediately.

Putting myself in my family's place was impossible. My mom's sister was her life, they were best friends and they talked every day – eleven months apart, they were practically twins. She has two boys, my mom has two boys. They were extremely close, closer than my mom and dad. And she's surrounded by the family and the family's mourning and everybody's doing what they do in that situation.

I tried to talk to my mom. I tried to stay in communication but they're in a hospital together, the whole family was together and I was the only one who wasn't there. I still apologize to her for not being there, but I know that I was in the right place. I was able to focus, to meditate, to almost pray at times, which is almost weird for me but I was in such a religious country that it kind of felt right to. I was able to confront it, to grab it, to look at it, to deal with it, and to work with it.

That's when I knew I needed to get my tattoo.

I'd thought about it before and it just made sense. I didn't exactly know why when I decided to, but between deciding to and making the appointment and then actually getting to the appointment six hours later all of the sense kind of caught up, and I realized why it was important that I do it. To put myself through the most painful thing I've experienced in my life, when my mom was going through the most painful experience of her life. It made sense. To… create this excruciating pain in the absence of pain. I say absence of pain, like, I'm not there mourning with my family, even if I'm upset and mourning, I'm still on vacation, I'm still doing things, I'm still living out a dream, I'm still in this beautiful area, I'm still riding a scooter through the jungle, you know, I'm not in hospital crying with my family for four days. So I guess I kind of, really welcomed the excruciating pain that it would bring.

The design inspiration was from the movie Papillon, the original one with Stevie McQueen, he got the butterfly on his chest. I was always in love with that movie. That dude was always so resilient, always on the move, and I loved that. As a kid I idolized Stevie, and so that tattoo's always been in the back of my head, like, it would be cool to do that one day. And then in Thailand it just made sense.

The butterfly has long been a symbol of reincarnation and the afterlife, as well as something that just floats above the earth gracefully. I continue to draw parallels with that time and the way that I felt to the butterfly on my chest. There was a moment where I realized that the butterfly will still float through the air with grace, even in the craziest of storms. And that was what I needed to do for my family, for my mom.

It's a traditional stick and poke tattoo or bamboo style, they did with a two-foot long steel rod, stuck it into my chest millions of times.

They had to switch artists through the tattoo – the first guy gave up because I was squirming too much. The second guy came in on a scooter with a boom box playing death metal, and there's all these stickers on his scooter and he's got gauges and tattoos. The first guy's just a nice-looking guy in a collared shirt, but the second guy you're like, 'that's a fucking tattoo artist'. Gauges, nerdy glasses, tons of tattoos, just fucking scrawny, looked like he played in a Thai thrash metal band. He came in, he was serious, he was fucking about business. He gave the assistant, I dunno, 500 baht, and that assistant went next door and bought him tobacco and rum and he rolled his cigarettes, took a shot of rum and got back into it.

They were just eating green mango, they had a plate with mango on it and they were just cutting chunks off and just eating it. So, every break we would take, I would go stand outside with my shirt off while I smoked a cigarette (I don't normally smoke cigarettes), drink rum and munch on this astringent, but weirdly satisfying, green mango dipped into spicy chili salt.

The pain was excruciating, and there were so many times I thought I can't take this shit. But the only thing that got me through was thinking of my cousins, thinking of my brother, thinking of my mom, thinking of my grandma. During the breaks, there were these Kiwi guys in this go-go bar across the street who kept trying to get me to come take shots with some hookers they were with. It felt like a weird nightmare. I should have been enjoying myself instead of getting poked and eating bitter fruit, but I was in too much pain. It was a well-rounded hurt. But at the same time it was a relief that I was able to experience that there rather than having to go through going to work and having to tell your friends why you're upset, seeing your family in pain, being with the person that's in more pain than you are and being with them for a long period of time.

Sometimes it's just easier to be away.

11/23/2·18

I made some food the other night and I had this crazy thought.

Sometimes when I'm at home I'll make just some sautéed kale with white beans and some chili flake and fresh lemon and throw an egg over the top and it's so simple and it's so delicious and it's become like a comfort staple for me, that I cook. And I was like, this could be my kids' comfort food. These, recipes and thoughts and little dishes and things that I do that I don't think of. I'm just like, I want some healthy food, but it can become my kids' comfort food – my family's food – generations down the line.

Food's pretty cool like that.

4. [Japan]

<u>My second trip this year was to Japan, and the first day, when
we went to Nancy Singleton Hachisu's, was the best.</u>

We took that bullet train out to the country. The train
pretty much had a view of Mount Fuji the whole time we
were heading out of the city through to the farm land and
countryside, which took a while, because Tokyo's pretty
immense. It's a huge city.

So, we finally get out to the country, we're pretty much lost
and we've gotta call a cab, which neither of us had done – it's
our second day in Tokyo and we don't know what the fuck's
going on. Luckily, these two Australians – Mel and Lim – our
saviors, were like, 'hey are you going to Nancy's? Do you want
to hop in a cab with us?'. They were fluent in Japanese and
got us out there.

Anyway, one of Nancy's first books was an inspiration to
me a long time ago, so to be where it was shot with the author
doing what was in the book was amazing. They were cooking
the rice over the fire in a traditional way in the backyard in a
big bamboo steamer, and they had the rice and the cloth
sacks and they just kept putting the rice in and letting it
cook, all the time drinking sake and beer and eating snacks.
The sake was home-brewed, thick and rice-y, the natto was
organic and home-fermented… we were experiencing all these
things I'd only ever dreamed of eating or have had, you know,
shitty versions of in the US, but had never really gotten to
experience properly.

We were there at New Year, a special time as it meant
that we were there for celebration, obviously, but also the
tradition of mochi making, where one family makes mochi
for the whole community so that everyone else doesn't have
to cook food during that period of celebration which is very
special to the Japanese.

A tribe Called Quest - Buggin' Out

Chasing Harvest

So, there's a community of people from the neighborhood and also from our community of chefs from around the world hanging out in Nancy's backyard around a fire, drinking, eating and using a fucking giant Donkey Kong hammer to smash cooked rice into a sweetened, thickened, gloopy awesome cloud of mochi that they put in, well, pretty much everything. I counted at least twelve different applications of mochi – from just taking mochi and putting it in a bowl of soup that Nancy made, to rolling it in sesame sugar and stuffing it with red bean paste (Nancy's mother-in-law, I think, showed me the way to roll it and everything). And it was pretty much transformed every time.

It was so great to immediately jump into the country and get a taste of what's in season, what's being preserved and what's happening – to get that taste of tradition and ritual immediately, but in that super familiar environment of hanging out in the backyard around a fire with a beer. Gathering in a yard, outside, even if it's winter, it's cold, and having some drinks, having some grog, with a spread of food and people helping themselves – that hospitality and that kind of experience with fire in the backyard, you know, whether it's a gas barbecue or a firepit or someone slowly shoveling logs onto a fire that's underneath this archaic rice cooker, um… it was all so new but so familiar at the same time. It was seriously cool.

Salmon hand rolls

Serves 4–6

Filling

½ lb (230 g) sushi-grade raw salmon,
  skin and bones removed
1 small Fuji apple, core removed and cut into cubes
4 red radishes, cut into cubes
1 scallion (spring onion), white and green parts
  finely sliced
1 teaspoon rice vinegar, plus extra if needed
1 teaspoon mirin
¼ teaspoon lemon zest
pinch of salt
2 tablespoons Extra-virgin Olive Oil Aïoli
  (see page 28)

To serve

freshly cooked sushi rice
toasted nori sheets, halved

One of the first meals we had in the house when I was in Japan was a build-your-own hand roll night. This was when everyone was arriving at the house and we were all getting there at different times. It was a really difficult place to find and there were all these streets, alleys and backroads that you could never imagine anyone driving down, then all of a sudden you were almost being hit by a car that's two feet wide.

Anyway, I wanted to make something that we could all kind of pick and chew at and just put out on the table, so I just got some sake from the local 7-11, a bunch of different ingredients from a local market and came back and everyone got on with making their own hand rolls. My favorite hand roll from that night – which was a night filled with a lot of sake, Japanese game shows on the TV and snacks – was this one, which had salmon mixed with crunchy radish, apple and creamy aïoli. It was really delicious.

Using a large chef's knife or cleaver, start by slicing the salmon into thin strips, then slice against the length of the strips to cut each strip into small, roughly equal pieces. Transfer the roughly minced salmon to a large bowl, add all of the remaining filling ingredients and mix together well. Taste and season with a little more salt and rice vinegar, if needed, then transfer to the fridge and leave to chill for a minimum of 30 minutes (or up to 2 hours).

When ready to eat, place a small amount of freshly cooked sushi rice onto a toasted nori sheet and gently spread it out evenly towards the edges. Working diagonally from the upper left corner to the center, spoon some of the salmon mixture over the rice, then fold the left bottom corner up towards the center before taking the upper right corner and wrapping it behind to make a cone shape. Consume immediately, so the nori doesn't get soggy.

Chasing Harvest

Coal-roasted sweet potatoes with tobiko aïoli

Serves 4–6

4 sweet potatoes, skin on
¾ cup (185 g/6½ oz) Extra-virgin Olive Oil Aïoli (see page 28)
pinch of sea salt
2 teaspoons togarashi seasoning
¼ cup (60 g/2 oz) tobiko, ikura or cured salmon roe
2 tablespoons sliced scallion (spring onion) tops

When I was in Japan it was really cold, so I'd get bundled up every morning and go for a run, both to help shake off the hangover and get out of the house, which would have eight or nine people in it, but mostly to explore the neighborhood. (When I travel I always like to run in a different direction each morning to explore where I'm at, and on this trip I was able to stumble on some cool little fish shops and produce shops as a result.) Every morning on the way home I would grab a couple of coal-roasted sweet potatoes from a sweet potato or yam vendor on the street who was just kind of sitting there bundled up in this steamy little corner outside of a convenience store. They'd be wrapped in the newspaper which was all in Japanese which was always fun to look at – and my cool down in the mornings would be to walk back with these warm sweet potatoes in my hands. Normally I'd just take them back and gnaw on them, or smash them and put a fried egg on top, but this version takes that idea a little bit further, using some of the ingredients I had back at the house to turn it into a bit of a riff on baked potato with all the fixin's.

Place a grill grate about 12 in (30 cm) above hot, glowing coals, or heat your grill (barbecue) to low.

Arrange the sweet potatoes on the grate and roast, turning occasionally, for 1 hour or until the potatoes are tender and a knife inserted into each comes out easily, but the skins have not blackened. (If it looks as though they are blackening too quickly, raise the rack slightly.)

Meanwhile, stir together the aïoli, salt and 1 teaspoon of togarashi in a bowl, then fold in the tobiko or other fish roe.

To serve, cut the soft sweet potatoes down the center and spread them open, then dollop over the aïoli and tobiko mixture. Sprinkle over the scallion tops and remaining togarashi to finish.

Braised daikon, mushies and greens

Serves 4

1 daikon radish (about 12 in/30 cm in length)
extra-virgin olive oil, for drizzling
4 cups (1 litre/34 fl oz) vegetable kombu stock
2 tablespoons miso paste
5½ oz (150 g) maitake, shiitake or oyster mushrooms,
    brushed clean
sea salt
1 handful of mizuna or young mustard green leaves
1 tablespoon rice vinegar

It's funny, but I didn't really have that crazy culinary experience that I was expecting to during my time in Japan, but one thing that did strike me was the excellence of the produce. All over the place there were markets and produce shops that were basically one man operations, and everybody who worked in them was very hospitable and welcoming. I enjoyed running in the morning, going into those shops and chatting and getting Japanese translations of the things that I loved to work with. Daikon was everywhere obviously – it being Japan – and it was winter, so mushrooms and mustard greens were too.

It was cold there and I was craving something brothy and braised, so one day I took a daikon back to the house and peeled it and popped it in the oven with the broth and just made some nice slices of it, then put it in the broth and put some mushrooms and greens over the top. It was more of an experiment, really, but it ended up being one of my favorite dishes that I made when I was in Japan.

Peel the daikon, trimming away the top and bottom. Cut the remainder into four equal-sized pieces.

Heat a splash of olive oil in a saucepan over medium–high heat, add the daikon pieces to the pan and cook for 4 minutes, turning, until lightly browned on all sides. Add the stock and miso paste and bring to a boil, then reduce the heat to a simmer, cover with a lid and cook, stirring occasionally, for 20–30 minutes or until the daikon is tender and a knife inserted comes out easily. Remove the pan from the heat leaving the daikon to sit in the hot broth.

Heat another splash of oil in a cast-iron frying pan over medium–high heat. Break the maitake mushroom clusters down into smaller pieces, add these to the pan and cook, stirring, for 5–6 minutes until golden brown and tender. Season with salt and set aside.

Meanwhile, toss the mizuna or mustard leaves together with the rice vinegar and another drizzle of olive oil.

To serve, remove the daikon pieces from the pan and cut into ¼ in (5 mm) slices. Divide the daikon slices among bowls, then ladle over the braising broth and drizzle over a little more olive oil to aromatize. Spoon over the cooked mushrooms and top with the dressed greens to finish.

In Tokyo, the food everywhere was insane. Just slurpy noodles all the time. There's a lot of street food but you're not supposed to eat in the street, so it's like, you buy it in the street and there's this little area in the street that's made for you to squat and eat. And then, although it's street food there's four garbage cans: one for excess broth; one for the bowls; one for the chopsticks and then one for regular trash. And a dude sitting there organizing the trash for, like, three dollar ramen that people are smashing in the streets. (I think the cheapest ramen were the best ones – the ones that I got on New Year's day on the street, the three dollar ones, they were probably my favorite.)

And then there's the markets. I had a really amazing moment at the vegetable market. I was buying things and getting excited about recognizing things and knowing what they were called, and the stall holder was equally excited to have some giant American dude who doesn't speak Japanese know that they are called 'shoshitos' and 'hoshigaki' and 'kaki' and things like that. And then he was, as I was picking things up he was telling me the name in Japanese and I was telling him the name in English and we were having this… having a moment together. And I was watching him run his shop and there were people coming out to the shop, to purchase things, give him lists of things and him being meticulously organized and extremely professional about selling vegetables. It was really awesome.

Other than that, one of the coolest things was, after the hike on Mount Takao, when we got soba with grated root. It seemed like that area was a very health-driven area because there were onsens and this big hike that you could go on, and lots of soba noodle restaurants around there and… there was that weird, starchy root that was grated into this pulp, paste that was put on top of the noodles and you'd stir it until it thickens the noodles and it was just like, an alien pulp that was on top of soba noodles that was delicious. I'm pretty sure it made me feel a little better.

One night, when we were having dinner I spent the time watching the Japanese businessmen eat at the adjacent table. I like to do that when I go out to eat in different countries, to watch people and just become a sponge and figure out what to do and what not to do, to figure out what they're doing and how to order. That was how I learnt to slurp noodles properly. Like, white people slurp noodles like you slurp spaghetti when you're a kid, but you don't actually breathe the noodle like they do in Japan.

So, learning the right way to slurp.

I went to Japan and I learnt how to slurp noodles and pound rice.

Japan wins Best Fast Food

Late-night slurpy noods

Serves 4

4 tablespoons soy sauce

2 tablespoons mirin

2 tablespoons rice vinegar

extra-virgin olive oil, for drizzling

8 chicken thighs, de-boned and cut into strips

6 scallion (spring onion) whites, cut into 1-in (2.5 cm) batons

1 tablespoon grated fresh ginger

1 tablespoon sesame seeds

14–16 oz (400–450 g) freshly cooked udon noodles

8 shiso leaves, torn

This came from my friends chanting 'slurpy noods, slurpy noods', because they were drunk in Tokyo winter and craving noodles that could be slurped up that were hot and belly warming. It's a super, super simple dish that is just easy, satisfying and – of course – slurpy.

Mix the soy, mirin, and rice vinegar together in a small bowl with a tablespoon of water. Set aside.

Heat a drizzle of extra-virgin olive oil in a large sauté pan or wok. When the pan is hot and the oil is near smoking, carefully add the chicken thigh strips and cook, stirring occasionally, for 3–4 minutes, or until the chicken starts to brown and is halfway cooked. Add the scallion batons and continue to cook, stirring, until the chicken is almost cooked through and the scallion is well caramelized.

Add the ginger and sesame seeds the pan and cook for a further 2–3 minutes, stirring frequently to prevent them from burning, then tip the noodles into the pan and pour over the soy sauce mixture. Toss everything together over the heat until the noodles have softened a little and absorbed the sauce, then remove from the heat, toss in the torn shiso leaves and serve immediately.

Chrysanthemum greens with garlic confit and chili honey

Serves 4

12 garlic cloves, peeled and halved
¼ cup (60 ml/2 fl oz) extra-virgin olive oil
1 bunch of chrysanthemum greens (also known as shungiku), washed and bottoms trimmed
pinch of sea salt
¼ cup (60 ml/2 fl oz) honey
1 teaspoon chili flakes

Chrysanthemum greens – also known as shungiku – were everywhere we went in Japan, where they are eaten both raw and cooked. I'm always stoked to cook a different kind of green, so I had a play with them while I was there, and this is the result. The greens have got a bit of bitterness to them, so the garlic confit here plays off of that, while the little bit of heat I've added here was probably a nod to the cold weather.

Blanch the halved garlic cloves in a saucepan of boiling salted water for 30 seconds, then strain. Repeat the process twice more, using fresh water each time, for a total of three times (this process will help remove the garlic's sharpness, leaving just the sweet flavor), then transfer the garlic cloves to a small saucepan set over a very low heat. Pour over enough olive oil to cover the garlic most of the way and leave to bubble away gently for at least 30 minutes.

Heat a drizzle of oil in a large frying pan over a medium heat, add the chrysanthemum greens and salt and cook for 4–6 minutes, stirring occasionally, until the greens are wilted and tender. Transfer the greens to a colander in the sink to let any excess moisture drain away, then tip them into a large serving bowl.

Stir the honey and chili flakes into the garlic confit, then pour the mix over the greens and toss well. Serve.

Postscript

I often think of that first time I headed off to Australia as like being the dude in the old-school circus that's got the helmet – his trick is that he's able to get shot out of the cannon and survive it and that's how I felt, you know, propelling down towards the ground with my fists out, getting ready to land and run and cook my ass off. Not really knowing what it was going to be like but having to be prepared and just, like, having to tuck away the emotion of leaving friends and family and you know, the things that make up a happy household and existence and a comfortable place, just walking away from that to kind of jettison yourself into the unknown. The known part was 'this is going to be really awesome work'. And it is. It was. But you don't really realize how much you sacrifice until later, in retrospect. The relationships you hurt, or end.

Now I feel it before I leave, and I'm tired of hurting people.

It's great to be a world-traveling chef. It's the dream, right? But there's a lot of shit people don't see or don't understand. Are you sure you want my job? Are you sure you want to be away from your friends and family and home? I mean, I'm sure there are people who do, but at the same time, do you live a mile away from your grandma? Do you love your Mom and Dad? Are your friends the best people in the whole world? Do you live in an amazing home, an amazing area?

I have a great life that I've started to figure out for myself out in Sacramento. I love it. And I leave it. Happily. Not for long. But at the end of the day it is, still, a sacrifice. Who'd want to be in a relationship with me when I'm away from home for six months of the year? Am I missing out on chances to meet that person because I'm gone so much, because I'm constantly moving?

You're either nomadic or you build a home. I'm putting off building a home to be nomadic. And I'm happy to be nomadic, for now, but eventually I want to evolve and have a home. And I worry that I'm going to have to sacrifice one for the other, eventually.

Right now it's pure bliss, confusion, adrenaline-fueled organized chaos and sandwiched between all that there's great food and entertaining which is at the core of my love of everything I do. But I wonder sometimes, how much sacrifice is worth it? And can you push it too far? Year after year after year if I keep sacrificing this time and I keep moving, will I even get to the point where I meet somebody to start a family with?

Because if I do start a family it's like, yeah great, you've traveled the world, you've gotten these experiences, you've stacked some chips, you're in a better place to start a family or whatever. But I do sometimes worry that one day I'm going to wake up and be 50 and I'll have seen the world, but I'll be utterly alone... Is that ok?

And these thoughts can start to twist my idea of another dream, you know. The dreams growing up – restaurant, Michelin stars, family. Rad wife. Not shit kids. The restaurant dream has already shattered and twisted and turned into whatever the fuck the dream is now, which I'm living and loving and doing but, will this new dream get shattered too? And will I be able to handle it if it does? Can you recover from that many dreams being shattered?

I don't know. I just don't know....

Recently, since getting back, I've been talking to my grandmas more about what their parents cooked, what they ate. You don't realize that it's important as a kid but so much of that is going to be lost.

My grandma's family utilized a communal larder. It wasn't a grocery store, but during the winter you would go in and you would donate what you grew and take what you needed from what other people grew. So, they'd have sacks of flour in there and although they didn't mill flour the neighbors may have done that and they'd put that in there. Jars of pickles, preserves, different things from their trees that they'd bring in to there. And you'd just leave what you could and take what you needed.

My great grandfather started that in Minnesota. In those bleak winters in Minnesota. It's pretty wild. I can only imagine walking into that and seeing what was in there and what it was like and what preserves were in jars and what kind of things were growing, and how they'd use them.

They were farmers. And they farmed a lot. And had a lot of cattle, a lot of livestock. And they would survive off of the cheap cuts of meat, the innards and everything. So my Grandma's got all these crazy German recipes and stuff, and I've got French recipes from my other grandma, along with different types of preservation techniques that they used in Nebraska for the root cellar, you know, tornado shelters and shit like that. Different ways of making chicken and dumplings, these old-school dishes.

I never thought these recipes were important as a kid, but now I realize I have to learn and understand that stuff to know where my roots are. Where home is, for me.

Anyway, there's a dish I want to do really bad that my grandma got made fun of for eating in school. Her breakfast was often soured milk pancakes. Basically buttermilk pancakes, but with soured milk. They'd make pancakes with it and then serve them with fried brains over the top. So I want to do a rendition with griddle cakes and sweetbreads, almost, perhaps even brains.

Maybe I'll try it tomorrow…

Because of her

Grandma's cottage cheese and apple butter

I think my grandma is responsible for teaching me patience in the kitchen, and the kitchen is responsible for teaching me patience in life. And that all stems from grandma's house. My brother and I cooked a lot of food at grandma's growing up; every time we went over there it was kind of like, 'Ok kids, what's the project – what are we making?'. Popcorn balls, fried chicken, the best mashed potatoes in the world, zucchini breads, chocolate chip cookies, doughnuts, cinnamon rolls… you name it, it was a young foodie's heaven.

We took our time with grandma – I honestly think that she put together projects that would take the better portion of the day so that we could stay focused! This cottage cheese we picked out of a book and it became one that we would do over and over at hers because we thought it was fun to watch something as familiar as milk turn into something as interesting as cottage cheese. We would also make jars and jars of apple butter – it was great to spend all day on it and end up with something we could put our names on, give as gifts and have the rest of the family enjoy. Grandma's slowed down on the apple butter production since and I don't think I'll ever be able to make mine as good as hers, but I'm trying to get close.

Cottage cheese
  (Makes approx. 2 cups/320 g/11½ oz)

1 gallon (4 litres/135 fl oz) whole (full-cream) milk
¾ cup (185 ml/6 fl oz) white vinegar
1½ teaspoons sea salt
a couple of cracks of black pepper
½ cup (125 ml/4 fl oz) heavy (thick/double) cream
  (optional)
drizzle of extra-virgin olive oil (optional)

Pour the milk into a large saucepan and set over a medium heat. Heat to 120°F (50°C), stirring occasionally, then remove from the heat and slowly pour in the vinegar. Stir for 1–2 minutes, then cover with a lid and leave to sit at room temperature for 30 minutes to allow the curds and whey to separate.

After 30 minutes, pour the mixture into a colander lined with cheesecloth (muslin) and leave it to drain for 5 minutes in the sink, then gather the corners of the cheesecloth, lift them up and gently squeeze the sides. Rinse the cheese 'bag' under cool running water for 3–5 minutes or until it is completely cooled, then transfer the contents to a mixing bowl and add the salt and pepper, stirring to combine and break up the curds and adding cream or a little extra-virgin olive oil if you like to soften the curds. This is best enjoyed fresh, though it will keep in an airtight container in the fridge for 2–3 days.

Tom Misch
Isn't she lovely

Apple butter (Makes approx. 9 cups/2.25 kg/5 lb)

4 lb (1.8 kg) apples, a mix of granny smith and
   gravenstein
2 cups (500 ml/17 fl oz) water
1 cup (250 ml/8½ fl oz) apple cider vinegar
approx. 4 cups (880 g/1 lb 15 oz) sugar
1 teaspoon ground cinnamon
½ teaspoon ground cloves
¼ teaspoon ground allspice
pinch of sea salt
zest and juice of 1 lemon

Quarter the apples, leaving the cores and skins intact
(this is where a lot of the necessary pectin comes from),
then add the pieces to a large saucepan or stockpot
together with the water and vinegar. Cover with a lid
and bring to a boil, then reduce to a simmer and cook
for 20–30 minutes until softened and falling apart.

Purée the apple by pressing the mixture through a
food mill or a fine-mesh sieve. Measure out the apple
mix, then transfer to a clean saucepan, adding ½ cup
(110 g/4 oz) of sugar to the pan for every cup of apple
pulp. Stir to dissolve the sugar and mix in the spices,
salt, lemon juice and zest.

Return the pot to the stovetop and cook the apple
butter over a medium–low heat, stirring occasionally and
scraping the bottom to prevent burning, for 1–1½ hours,
or until thick and smooth. To test doneness, place a small
quantity on to a plate. When no rim of liquid separates
from the edge of the apple butter, it's done (Grandma
would also do that same test on a wooden spoon).
Pour into clean, sterilized jars, where it will keep for ages.

Index

Acknowledgments

I'm astounded by the amount of work that goes into a project like this and seriously honored to have been able to work with such talented, dedicated and creative minds. If you ever see me in person and want to talk about this book, please ask about the people that helped me, so that I may tell their story.

Thank you to the Hardie Grant team of wizards that worked on this book – the times spent chasing the harvest with y'all have been an unforgettable joy. Bless you for understanding me, asking the right questions, and putting up with me. Snake Farm forever.

My family at Cobram Estate has been instrumental in every bit of my success. Thank you for turning my world on its head and giving me the opportunities to not only do the things I love, but to also discover and explore new passions. I so value the thread of authenticity that runs through everyone at Cobram and the shared dedication to greatness is nothing short of inspirational. Your trust means the world to me. Thank you.

I'm beyond lucky to have my life and food captured by a couple of the most astonishing humans that have come in to my life. Luisa Brimble, BOOMPOW!! I miss you every day until I see you again, you've been a warm light in my life since the moment I met you. Thank you for your endless range of talents, stories, encouragement and the best hugs ever. You're a star. Melissa Gayle Gustafson, thank you for being such a large piece of this journey. To the early mornings, late nights, letting me vent, and offering guidance with heart and purity on another level. I can't wait to see Winter become the best big sister, which should be happening any day now! You got the vibe, mama. Your talents have spawned a new level of inspiration. I'm blind without the two of you.

I'm grateful for the decades of love and support from my family and friends. I love the shit out of all of you. My brother, you're a saint for not kicking me out when I couldn't pay rent but kept throwing dinner parties and being a piece of garbage. All of my aunts act as my board of advisors and I must say, their unconditional love has been the comforting net I am relieved to know I can fall back on at any time of my life.

My friends are my constant inspiration, my happiness, and my energy – without you guys I'm lifeless. I owe you everything.

To every olive tree growing on this earth and the Goddess Athena… cheers.

Last but certainly not least… thank you Hazel Levengood. I'm eternally sorry for any time I've ever yelled at you. I still really can't believe what we've been through, but I'm so grateful we've come out this way. You've been my muse, my driving force of dedication, my rock, and my best friend. None of this would have ever happened without you. I'd do it all over again in a heartbeat. You're the best.

Published in 2020 by Hardie Grant Books, an imprint of Hardie Grant Publishing.

Hardie Grant Books (Melbourne)
Building 1, 658 Church Street
Richmond, Victoria 3121

Hardie Grant Books (London)
5th & 6th Floors,
52–54 Southwark Street
London SE1 1UN
hardiegrantbooks.com

A Prepublication Data Service entry is available from the catalogue of the National Library of Australia at www.nla.gov.au

Chasing Harvest
ISBN 9781743796498

Publishing management by Courtney Nicholls
Edited by Simon Davis
Art Direction by Vaughan Mossop
Designed by NBHD Creative
Commissioned photography by Luisa Brimble and Melissa Gayle
Colour reproduction by Splitting Image Colour Studio
Printed in China by Leo Paper Group